Taxcafe.co.uk Tax Guides

Tax Planning for Directors

By Carl Bayley BSc FCA

Important Legal Notices:

Taxcafe®
Tax Guide - "Tax Planning for Directors"

Published by:
Taxcafe UK Limited
67 Milton Road
Kirkcaldy KY1 1TL
Tel: (0044) 01592 560081
Email: team@taxcafe.co.uk

ISBN 978-1-911020-74-5

1st edition, January 2022

Disclaimer
Before reading or relying on the content of this tax guide please read the disclaimer.

Disclaimer

1. This guide is intended as **general guidance** only and does NOT constitute accountancy, tax, investment or other professional advice.

2. The author and Taxcafe UK Limited make no representations or warranties with respect to the accuracy or completeness of this publication and cannot accept any responsibility or liability for any loss or risk, personal or otherwise, which may arise, directly or indirectly, from reliance on information contained in this publication.

3. Please note that tax legislation, the law and practices of Government and regulatory authorities (e.g. HM Revenue & Customs) are constantly changing. We therefore recommend that for accountancy, tax, investment or other professional advice, you consult a suitably qualified accountant, tax adviser, financial adviser, or other professional adviser.

4. Please also note that your personal circumstances may vary from the general examples provided in this guide and your professional adviser will be able to provide specific advice based on your personal circumstances.

5. This guide covers UK taxation only and any references to 'tax' or 'taxation', unless the contrary is expressly stated, refer to UK taxation only. Please note that references to the 'UK' do not include the Channel Islands or the Isle of Man. Foreign tax implications are beyond the scope of this guide.

6. All persons described in the examples in this guide are entirely fictional. Any similarities to actual persons, living or dead, or to fictional characters created by any other author, are entirely coincidental.

7. The views expressed in this publication are the author's own personal views and do not necessarily reflect the views of any organisation he may represent.

About the Author

Carl Bayley is the author of a series of 'Plain English' tax guides designed specifically for the layman and non-specialist. His aim is to help business owners, landlords, and families understand the taxes they face and make savings through sensible planning and by having confidence to know what they can claim. Carl's speciality is his ability to take the weird, complex world of taxation and set it out in the kind of clear, straightforward language taxpayers can understand. As he often says, "My job is to translate 'tax' into English."

Carl enjoys his role as a tax author, as he explains, "Writing these guides gives me the opportunity to use the skills and knowledge learned over more than thirty years in the tax profession for the benefit of a wider audience. The most satisfying part of my success as an author is the chance to give the average person the same standard of information as the 'big guys' at a price everyone can afford."

Carl takes the same approach when speaking on taxation, a role he undertakes with great enthusiasm, including his highly acclaimed annual 'Budget Breakfast' for the Institute of Chartered Accountants. In addition to being a recognised author and speaker, Carl has spoken on taxation on radio and television, including the BBC's 'It's Your Money' programme and BBC Radio 2's Jeremy Vine Show.

Carl began his career as a Chartered Accountant in 1983 with one of the 'Big 4' accountancy firms. After qualifying as a double prize-winner, he began specialising in taxation. He worked for several major international firms until beginning the new millennium by launching his own practice, through which he provided advice on a variety of taxation issues; especially property taxation, inheritance tax, and tax planning for small and medium-sized businesses, for twenty years, before deciding to focus exclusively on his favourite role as author and presenter.

Carl is a former Chairman of the Tax Faculty of the Institute of Chartered Accountants in England and Wales and a member of the Institute's governing Council. He is also a former President of ICAEW Scotland and member of the ICAEW Board. He has co-organised the annual Practical Tax Conference since its inception in 2002.

Aside from his tax books, Carl is an avid creative writer. He is currently waiting for someone to have the wisdom to publish his debut novel, while he works on the rest of the series. When he isn't working, he takes on the equally taxing challenges of hill walking and horse riding: his Munro tally is now 106 and, while he remains a novice rider, his progress is cantering along nicely. Carl lives in the Scottish Borders, where he enjoys spending time with his partner, Linda. He has three children and his first grandchild arrived in April 2021.

Dedication & Thanks

For the Past,

To Diana, the memory of your love warms me still. Thank you for bringing me into the light and making it all possible. To Arthur, your wise words still come back to guide me; and to my loving grandmothers, Doris and Winifred.

Between you, you left me with nothing I could spend, but everything I need.

Also to my beloved friends: Mac, William, Edward, Rusty, Dawson, and the grand old lady, Morgan. Thank you for all those happy miles; I still miss you all.

For the Present,

To the lovely lady Linda, one of the front line heroes of the past two years: bless you princess, I'm so proud of you. Thank you for bringing the sunshine back into my life, for opening my ears, and putting the song back in my heart. How quickly and completely you have become my world: I owe you more than you will ever know.

Also to Ollie, the world's oldest puppy: thank you for these happy miles.

For the Future,

To James, a true twenty-first century gentleman and one of the nicest guys I have ever met. To Robert, the 'chip off the old block', who is both cursed and blessed to have inherited a lot of my character; luckily for him, there is a lot of his mother in him too! And to Michelle, one of the most interesting people I have ever met. I am so very proud of every one of you and I can only hope I, in turn, will be able to leave each of you with everything you need.

Finally, to Sebastian: welcome to the world, wee man.

Thanks are due to:

The Taxcafe team, past and present, for their help in making these books far more successful than I could ever have dreamed; my old friend and mentor, Peter Rayney, for his inspiration and for showing me tax and humour can mix; Rebecca, Paul, and David for taking me into the fold at the Tax Faculty, and for their fantastic support at our practical tax conference over many years.

And last, but far from least, thanks to Nick for giving me the push!

C.B., Roxburghshire, January 2022

Contents

Chapter 1

Introduction

Small company owners (or 'owner/directors') face a huge number of tax changes over the next couple of years. For the most part, they will be facing tax increases, although there are a few tiny morsels of good news amid the gloom.

In this guide, I will explain these tax changes and help you understand what they mean for you and your company. While it is mostly bad news, forewarned is forearmed, so it's important to know what is coming your way.

But it's not just about being a passive victim; I am also going to look at how you can plan to mitigate the impact of the changes through sensible tax planning measures. We will revisit and reassess some of the most important tax planning areas for small companies and their directors and examine how the changes ahead affect them. I will show you when and how the tax planning strategies that work well at the moment need to be adapted to cater for the changing environment.

As you progress through the guide, you will see some things will stay the same, and some will change. It's important to keep on top of the changes if you are going to keep as much of your company's hard-earned profits as possible.

After this introductory chapter, I will summarise the tax changes affecting small company owners in Chapter 2, where I will also begin to analyse their impact.

In Chapter 3, we will begin to look at the tax planning implications of the changes, and I will also introduce the important tax planning concept of marginal tax rates.

Chapters 4 and 5 cover the one of the most critical areas of tax planning for small company owners: profit extraction. We will start by reaffirming some important guiding principles then address the age-old question of 'salary or dividends', before rounding off with a review of other useful ways to take money out of your company tax efficiently, and how they stand up to the tax changes ahead. Some of them come out rather well!

Chapter 6 follows on by looking at the concept of 'pay now, save later' where we will see how a little pain now may lead to a big gain in future. Long-term planning is the key to extracting company profits as tax efficiently as possible.

The Government's tax increases will lead to a general increase in the cost of employment, and this comes on top of other pressures on employers struggling to recruit or retain staff. In Chapter 7, we will look at what measures you can take to combat the increased cost of employing your staff.

The increases in tax rates for both small companies and their directors over the next few years have important implications for year end tax planning. Chapters 8 to 11 cover this subject in detail. I have broken the subject down into multiple chapters because the critical dates for the planning vary, depending on what we are looking at. I believe this approach should make it easier for readers to understand what they need to do and when, including paying dividends, other action to take by 5th April 2022, and planning around the company's own accounting date.

When it comes to capital expenditure, the planning is also dependent on many other factors, which is why Chapter 11 is devoted to explaining all the issues to consider.

Finally, in Chapter 12, we wind up our review of the tax changes by looking at the most fundamental issue of all: is it still worth using a company? Some of the results may surprise you!

Spouses and Civil Partners

For the purposes of this guide, a 'spouse' includes a civil partner, but only includes spouses who are legally married (or legally registered civil partners). Similarly, a 'married couple' refers only to legally married couples or registered civil partners. Unmarried couples are subject to different rules for tax purposes.

Scottish Taxpayers

Different Income Tax rates and thresholds apply to Scottish taxpayers on most forms of income, including salaries.

However, Scottish taxpayers have the same personal allowance as other UK residents and pay the same rates of Income Tax on dividends, interest, and other savings income. They also pay National Insurance at the same rates and will be subject to the Health and Social Care Levy in the same way as other UK residents. Furthermore, Scottish companies are subject to Corporation Tax at the same rates as other companies.

Hence, the vast majority of the material in this guide applies equally to Scottish companies and their owners, with only some minor differences in respect of salaries paid to Scottish taxpayers.

Assumptions in this Guide

Throughout this guide (including all examples), unless specifically stated to the contrary, it is assumed all individuals are:

i)   UK resident and domiciled for tax purposes
ii) Not subject to the Child Benefit Charge
iii) Not claiming the marriage allowance (see Appendix A)
iv) Not Scottish taxpayers (see above)

It is also assumed, unless specifically stated to the contrary, that all companies:

i)   Are UK resident for tax purposes
ii) Are wholly or mainly engaged in trading activities or in letting property to unconnected persons
iii) Prepare accounts for a period of twelve months
iv) Have no associated companies
v)   Are not trading in the banking, oil, or gas sectors

It is additionally assumed the UK tax regime will remain unchanged in the future, except to the extent of announcements already made at the time of publication.

Inflation

I have also made various assumptions about inflation for the purposes of the examples, calculations, and tables in this guide. I will explain these as we progress. I'm afraid I don't have a crystal ball, so I cannot promise anything about the accuracy of these assumptions.

However, we know inflation has seen a sharp increase in recent months and, combining this with the Government's five year freeze for most tax allowances and thresholds, means we need to make some sort of assumption in order to assess the impact of the Government's measures in real terms.

I, for one, am also firmly convinced that real inflation, the kind that hits people's pockets week in, week out, is much better represented by the retail prices index, 'RPI', rather than the Government's more favoured, but less realistic, consumer prices index, 'CPI'.

Even when the Government does increase tax thresholds, it uses the CPI as the measure of inflation, meaning those increases generally still do not keep pace with real inflation per the RPI. I have reflected this difference in some parts of the guide, although in others I have kept it simple and used a single rate of inflation for everything. I will make my assumptions clear, so you can decide for yourself what the true position is likely to be. Like I said, I do not have a crystal ball!

Chapter 2

Change is Upon Us

Directors and their companies face an enormous number of tax changes over the next couple of years. These changes will have a profound effect on companies' after tax profits and on directors' personal tax liabilities.

The pandemic has led to unprecedented levels of Government borrowing. Paying back the vastly swollen public debt inevitably means tax increases and, while these are happening across the board, a large part of the burden is falling on companies and their directors.

In this chapter, I will provide a summary of the tax changes, and begin to examine the impact they will have on small companies and their directors. Later in the guide, I will take a more detailed look at how some key aspects of tax planning for small companies and directors are affected by the changes.

The Corporation Tax Increase

Most companies currently pay Corporation Tax at the single rate of 19%. However, the main rate of Corporation Tax will increase, by almost a third, to 25% from 1st April 2023.

If your company makes annual profits of at least £250,000 and you have a 31st March accounting date, that's pretty much the end of the story. In other cases, however, there are a few complications to be aware of.

For companies with other accounting date, transitional rules will apply to the accounting period that spans 1st April 2023.

Example
Seacon Ltd makes a profit of £300,000 for the year ending 31st December 2023. It will pay Corporation Tax as follows:

For period from 1st January to 31st March 2023:

£300,000 x 90/365 = £73,973 @ 19% =   £14,055

For period from 1st April to 31st December 2023:

£300,000 x 275/365 = £226,027 @ 25% =   £56,507

Total for year ending 31st December 2023:   £70,562

The company's effective Corporation Tax rate is 23.521%: the same rate will apply to any company drawing up accounts for the year ending 31st December 2023 with a profit of £250,000 or more.

If Seacon Ltd continues to make profits of £250,000 or more, it will pay Corporation Tax at a simple flat rate of 25% for the year ending 31st December 2024 and subsequent years.

The transitional rules applying to periods spanning 1st April 2023 mean some companies will begin to suffer an increase in their Corporation Tax rate as early as May 2022.

Smaller Companies

Companies with annual profits not exceeding a 'lower limit' of £50,000 will continue to pay Corporation Tax at 19%. This rate will be termed the 'small profits rate'.

Companies with annual profits between £50,000 and £250,000 will also pay a reduced rate of Corporation Tax, somewhere between 19% and 25%. This will be achieved by applying a system of marginal relief to companies with annual profits falling between the lower limit of £50,000 and an upper limit of £250,000.

Marginal relief will be given at a rate of 3/200ths on the amount by which profits are less than the upper limit, as illustrated by this example.

Example
Geolaz Ltd makes a profit of £180,000 for the year ending 31st March 2024. Its profit is therefore £70,000 less than the upper limit. The company's Corporation Tax bill is calculated as follows:

£180,000 x 25% =	*£45,000*
Less Marginal Relief	
£70,000 x 3/200 =	*(£1,050)*
Corporation Tax due	*£43,950*

In this case, the company's overall effective Corporation Tax rate is 24.417%.

The marginal relief system creates an effective marginal Corporation Tax rate of 26.5% on profits falling between the lower and upper limits.

Hence for companies with twelve month accounting periods beginning after 31st March 2023, and no associated companies, a simpler way to look at the new regime is to say there are three Corporation Tax rate bands, as follows:

Profits	CT Rate	
Up to £50,000	19%	Small profits rate
£50,000 to £250,000	26.5%	Marginal rate
Over £250,000	25%	Main rate

The Government will never mention the marginal rate of 26.5%, you won't see it on any official Government websites, but for companies with profits falling into this band it is a reality that is critical to their tax planning.

To prove the validity of this simpler approach, let's return to the previous example.

Example Revisited

Geolaz Ltd's Corporation Tax calculation for the year ending 31st March 2024 can alternatively be expressed as follows:

£50,000 @ 19% =	*£9,500*
£130,000 @ 26.5% =	*£34,450*
Total	*£43,950*

Simpler calculation: same result. It works in the vast majority of cases, though not all.

Associated Companies & Other Issues

The lower and upper limits must be amended appropriately where accounts are drawn up for a period other than twelve months. For example, the upper and lower limits for a nine month (275 day) accounting period ending on 31st December 2023 will be £187,842 (£250,000 x 275/366) and £37,568 (£50,000 x 275/366) respectively.

Why 366 not 365? Corporation Tax is based on Financial Years ending on 31st March. The 2023 Financial Year, ending on 31st March 2024, has 366 days.

The lower and upper limits are also reduced where the company has any associated companies: broadly other companies controlled by the same person or group of persons. One associated company means the limits are halved, two associated companies means they are divided by three... and so on.

Small private companies (known as 'close companies') that are not wholly or mainly carrying on qualifying activities are not entitled to the 19% small profits rate or marginal relief. Fortunately, most companies are carrying on a qualifying business as this includes a trade and property letting to unconnected third parties.

Companies are not subject to Corporation Tax on any dividend income they receive. However any dividend income from external investments (i.e. not from a group company) will lead to a reduction in marginal relief.

For a full, detailed explanation of the Corporation Tax increase, see the Taxcafe.co.uk guide 'The Company Tax Changes'.

The Big Freeze

The Government has frozen Income Tax bands and thresholds at their current levels until 5th April 2026 (i.e. until the 2025/26 tax year).

This may not sound like a change, but it is. Income Tax bands and thresholds normally increase in line with inflation each year. This means the real value of the bands and thresholds is usually maintained. However, the freeze means the true value of the bands will be eroded by inflation.

For example, the higher rate tax threshold is currently £50,270 and will still be £50,270 in 2025/26. If inflation averages 3.5% over the period of the freeze, the real value of the higher rate tax threshold by 2025/26 will be just £43,800 in today's terms. We will take a further look at the impact of the big freeze on small company owners in Chapter 6.

This is important to company directors as it will affect the tax they pay on any salary or dividends they take from the company. It will also affect the company's employees' take home pay, leading to upward pressure on wages.

National Insurance Increases

All National Insurance rates are being increased by 1.25% from 6th April 2022. This will affect directors in a number of ways in 2022/23.

Firstly, as the employer, the company will pay secondary Class 1 National Insurance on employee wages and salaries in excess of £9,880 (or £190 per week) at the rate of 15.05% (up from the current rate of 13.8%).

Secondly, the company's employees will also suffer a 1.25% increase in their own National Insurance burden, leading to further upward pressure on wages.

Taken together these first two points mean there will be a 2.5% increase in the tax cost of employing people. We will look at some potential ways to combat this in Chapter 7.

Thirdly, any salary the director takes in excess of £9,100 will be subject to employer's secondary National Insurance at 15.05% (up from 13.8%).

Fourthly, any salary the director takes in excess of £9,880 will be subject to employee's primary Class 1 National Insurance: at 13.25% on amounts up to £50,270 (up from 12%), and at 3.25% on any excess (up from 2%).

A further knock-on effect will be an increase in the National Insurance charge on any taxable benefits in kind provided to the company's employees (e.g. company cars, private health care, etc). Benefits provided to the directors themselves will also be subject to higher National Insurance charges, including the deemed benefit in kind on beneficial loans.

Exemptions and Reliefs

All of the above is subject to the following reliefs and exemptions:

- Directors and other employees over state pension age are exempt from primary Class 1 National Insurance
- Each employer is entitled to deduct a £4,000 employment allowance against the cost of employer's secondary National Insurance each year: except companies where one director is the only paid employee and employers with an annual National Insurance bill in excess of £100,000
- Salaries paid to employees aged under 16 are not subject to either primary or secondary National Insurance
- Salaries up to £50,270 paid to employees aged under 21, or apprentices under 25, are exempt from employer's National Insurance
- Further reliefs apply to ex-service personnel in their first year back on 'civvy street' and employees working predominantly within designated Freeport sites

A Thorn by any Other Name

We at Taxcafe have always said National Insurance is simply extra Income Tax. It has often been used as a way to raise tax that is seen as being more 'palatable' to the electorate because of its association with pension entitlement and the NHS. But, as far as we are concerned, it really is just extra tax.

Now the Government is taking this long-running deception to a new level. From 6th April 2023, the National Insurance increase will be hived off, separated into a different tax, and rebranded as the Health and Social Care Levy.

In my view, this is simply a way for the Government to be able to claim, at the next General Election, that they didn't really increase National Insurance in direct contravention of their manifesto pledge at the last election. Why, oh why can't they just be honest and admit they've had to tear up the manifesto because of the pandemic?

The rebranded Health and Social Care Levy will apply in 2023/24 and later years in almost exactly the same way as the National Insurance increase will apply in 2022/23: with one very important exception, and possibly a few other variations we are not yet certain about.

The important exception is that the Health and Social Care Levy will apply to directors and employees over state pension age.

Another issue which is yet to be clarified is whether the £4,000 employment allowance can be set against the Health and Social Care Levy. If not, even the smallest companies will face a cost in taking on many employees.

The only good news is the Government has confirmed the other exemptions and reliefs from employer's National Insurance described above (employees aged under 21, apprentices under 25, ex-service personnel, and employees in Freeports) will apply to the Health and Social Care Levy in the same way as National Insurance.

Dividend Tax Increase

As we all know, the Government pledged not to increase Income Tax rates before the next General Election. Many might excuse them for having to go back on their manifesto pledge under current circumstances, but it's worth pointing out this pledge was repeated by Chancellor Rishi Sunak in the March 2021 Budget when he said, "This Government is not going to raise the rates of Income Tax, National Insurance, or VAT."

However, not only did they lie to us about their plans for National Insurance, they are also putting up Income Tax on dividends. For some bizarre reason, dividends seem to be another exception that allows them to break their promises.

From 6th April 2022, the Income Tax rates on dividend income will increase by 1.25%. The current three band system will continue, with dividends always being regarded as the top part of an individual's income.

The dividend allowance which exempts up to £2,000 of dividend income each tax year will remain at that level for 2022/23 and, as far as we know, for the foreseeable future thereafter, although this cannot be guaranteed.

It is important to remember, the dividend allowance applies to all your dividend income in the tax year, not just dividends from your own company. Hence, if you receive £500 in dividends from stock market investments, you can only pay yourself £1,500 in tax-free dividends from your own company under the dividend allowance.

Putting this all together, the Income Tax rates on dividend income this year and next can broadly be described as follows:

Income Band	2021/22	2022/23
Up to £14,570 (1)	0%	0%
£14,570 to £50,270	7.5%	8.75%
£50,270 to £100,000	32.5%	33.75%
£100,000 to £125,140 (2)/(3)	48.75%	50.625%
£125,140 to £150,000	32.5%	33.75%
Over £150,000	38.1%	39.35%

Remember, dividends are always the top part of your income but the first £2,000 of all dividends received in the tax year are tax-free (subject to Notes 3 and 5 below). Hence, for example, if you have other taxable income of £50,000 in 2022/23 and also pay yourself a dividend of £20,000, the first £2,000 will be tax-free but the remaining £18,000 will be taxed at 33.75%.

Notes

1. £14,570 represents the sum of the £12,570 personal allowance and the £2,000 dividend allowance. This is the maximum tax-free dividend an individual with no other taxable income can receive.
2. These effective tax rates are created by the withdrawal of the personal allowance from individuals with income over £100,000 (at the rate of £1 of lost allowance for each £2 of income over the threshold). The rates given in the table apply where the individual has no other taxable income. Where the individual does have other taxable income, the rates may be 52.5% (for 2021/22) and 53.75% (for 2022/23), or even as much as 55% (for 2021/22) and 56.25% (for 2022/23).

3. Dividends covered by the dividend allowance that fall in this income band are not tax free. While the dividend itself is not directly taxed, it still causes the withdrawal of the personal allowance, creating an effective tax rate of 20%.

4. Directors who have the highest taxable income in a household with children qualifying for child benefit will suffer the Child Benefit Charge on income falling in the band between £50,000 and £60,000. Even with just one qualifying child, the tax rate on dividends falling into the band of income between £50,270 and £60,000 is 43.5% in 2021/22 and 45.1% in 2022/23. With more qualifying children, the effective tax rate will be greater.

5. Where the director is subject to the Child Benefit Charge, dividends covered by the dividend allowance will still count as income for the purposes of the charge and hence will still give rise to a tax liability.

We will take a closer look at the impact of the dividend tax increases on profit extraction strategies for directors in Chapter 4, and on year-end planning for 5th April 2022 in Chapter 8.

Director's Loans

In addition to the 1.25% increase in the employer's National Insurance charge on beneficial loans to directors outstanding after 5th April 2022, new loans made after that date and still outstanding nine months after the company's accounting date will attract a Corporation Tax charge (known as a 'Section 455 charge') of 33.75%.

Loans made before 6th April 2022, are subject to a Section 455 Corporation Tax charge of 32.5%.

While the rate used for the Section 455 charge is linked to the Income Tax rate on dividends received by higher rate taxpayers, the same rate applies regardless of the level of taxable income received by the individual.

We will look at some of the planning implications of this tax increase in Chapters 5 and 9.

Is It All Bad News?

Mostly, I'm afraid it is. But there has been some good news on the capital allowances front.

The temporary increase in the maximum limit for the annual investment allowance to £1m has been further extended to 31st March 2023. We will take a closer look at the implications for small companies in Chapter 11.

In the March 2021 Budget, the Chancellor announced the introduction of a super-deduction of 130% for qualifying expenditure on new plant and machinery made by companies between 1st April 2021 and 31st March 2023. In addition to the requirement that the expenditure must be on new items (not second hand), a number of other restrictions apply, including (as usual) an exclusion for cars.

In addition to the super-deduction, a first year allowance of 50% will be available for the same period in respect of new integral features and other new assets (excluding cars) that would normally fall into the special rate pool and only attract a writing down allowance of 6%.

We will look at some of the planning implications of the super-deduction in Chapter 11. For a more detailed examination of the topic, see the Taxcafe.co.uk guide *'The Company Tax Changes'*.

What Does It All Mean?

The numerous tax changes faced by small companies and directors over the coming years warrant a detailed review of many tax planning strategies, including profit extraction for company owners, year-end planning (both for the tax year and the company's accounting year), tax-efficient remuneration for employees, and capital allowances planning. In the coming chapters, I will guide you through that review and look at how to mitigate the impact of the tax increases for your company and yourself.

But first, let's look at the impact of these changes on a typical small(ish) company without undertaking any tax planning.

Example Part 1: Current Year (2021/22)
Maud and Adam are the owners and directors of Rogmoo Ltd. In the year ending 31st March 2022, the company makes a profit of £587,638 before paying wages of £25,000 each to ten staff and salaries of £9,568 (the National Insurance threshold) each to Maud and Adam.

Each staff member suffers combined Income Tax and National Insurance of £4,338 on their wages for the year, leaving them with net take home pay of £20,662, or £397.35 per week.

The company suffers employer's National Insurance of £18,502 on its wages and salaries, bringing its profit before tax down to £300,000. Maud and Adam set aside £63,000 for working capital and £57,000 to settle the company's Corporation Tax bill then pay themselves dividends of £180,000, or £90,000 each. After paying the resultant Income Tax of £18,199 each, and including their salaries, this leaves each of them with net after tax income of £81,368, or a total of £162,738 as a couple.

For the sake of illustration, I am assuming the company has sufficient accumulated reserves to pay the dividends described and that Maud and Adam are able to do all the necessary calculations in time to pay their dividends by 5th April 2022. In practice, of course, this would probably take a little longer and there would be some time lag before the dividends were paid. Nonetheless, the example remains a valid illustration of a typical small company and its owner's current position.

Auto-enrolment pensions have also been ignored for the sake of illustration: let's just say everyone opted out.

So what happens next year (2022/23) without any planning?

We know the primary National Insurance threshold will increase to £9,880, and the secondary threshold to £9,100. We know the personal allowance and all other Income Tax thresholds will remain the same. We also know about the increases in the National Insurance rates, although the Corporation Tax increase will not impact on Rogmoo Ltd yet.

Let's also assume the company's profits before paying wages and salaries will increase in line with inflation at 3.5%, as will the amount Maud and Adam need to set aside for additional working capital.

Finally, let's assume Maud and Adam want to ensure their loyal workforce receive the same amount in weekly net take home pay in real terms.

With inflation at 3.5% this would amount to £411.26, but because of the National Insurance increase and the freeze in the personal allowance, their gross wages will need to increase by much more than 3.5% to achieve this. In fact, each employee will need gross wages of £26,310 for the year, an increase of 5.24%.

Example Part 2: Next Year (2022/23)
In the year ending 31st March 2023, Rogmoo Ltd makes a profit of £608,205 before paying wages of £26,310 each to its ten staff and salaries of £9,880 each to Maud and Adam. The company suffers a total of £22,137 in employer's National Insurance at 15.05%, leaving it with a profit before tax of £303,204.

Maud and Adam set aside £65,205 for working capital and £57,609 to settle the company's Corporation Tax bill then pay themselves dividends of £180,390, or £90,195 each. After paying the resultant Income Tax of £19,446 each, and including their salaries, this leaves each of them with net after tax income of £80,629, or a total of £161,258 as a couple.

In absolute terms, Maud and Adam are £1,480 worse off, but if we adjust for inflation, the £161,258 received next year is equivalent to a current value of £155,805, leaving them £6,933 poorer in real terms. And that's just the beginning.

In the following year (2023/24), the National Insurance increase will be rebranded as the Health and Social Care Levy but its impact will remain the same. Much worse though is the fact Rogmoo Ltd's Corporation Tax rate will increase to 25%.

I am also going to assume the following amounts again increase in line with inflation at 3.5%:

- The company's profit before wages and salaries
- The staff's net weekly take home pay
- The amount Maud and Adam need to set aside for additional working capital
- The primary National Insurance threshold
- The secondary National Insurance threshold

The increases in the National Insurance thresholds mirror the Government's behaviour this year, although they are far from certain of taking place.

Example Part 3: The Following Year (2023/24)

In the year ending 31st March 2024, Rogmoo Ltd makes a profit of £629,492 before paying wages of £273,595 in total to its staff and salaries of £10,244 each to Maud and Adam. The company suffers a total of £23,168 in employer's National Insurance and Health and Social Care Levy, leaving it with a profit before tax of £312,241.

Maud and Adam set aside £67,487 for working capital and £78,060 to settle the company's Corporation Tax liability at 25%. This leaves only £166,694 available to pay dividends, or £83,347 each. After paying the resultant Income Tax of £17,245 each, and including their salaries, this leaves each of them with net after tax income of £76,346, or a total of £152,692 as a couple.

In absolute terms, Maud and Adam are now £10,046 worse off than they were in 2021/22. Adjusting for compound inflation totalling 7.12% over two years, they are actually more than £20,000 poorer in real terms.

If we follow this model for the remaining two years of the Government's freeze in Income Tax thresholds, we see the couple's net after tax income declining in real terms (at current value), as follows:

	Absolute Terms	**Real Terms**
2021/22 (current)	£162,738	£162,738
2022/23	£161,258	£155,805
2023/24	£152,692	£142,540
2024/25	£156,246	£140,925
2025/26	£159,964	£139,399

It's sobering isn't it? And I don't think Maud and Adam are particularly unusual, especially given the difficulties many businesses are experiencing in recruiting and retaining staff, meaning employers must respond to maintain, or even increase, net take home pay in real terms.

One could argue that they could set less aside for working capital, but that would inevitably lead to increased borrowing and reduced profits in future.

That's why small company owners need to plan: and that's what we're going to look at in the following chapters.

Chapter 3

Tax Planning Implications

The tax changes we looked at in Chapter 2 have a huge number of tax planning implications. In the following chapters, we will focus on some issues of particular importance for small companies and their directors. In this chapter, I would first like to make a few general points.

Marginal Tax Rates

A lot of tax planning is about marginal tax rates. A marginal tax rate is a measure of the additional tax suffered on each additional £1 of income, or the amount of tax saved on each additional £1 of tax deductible expenditure, or tax relief, claimed.

Effective marginal tax rates are not always the same as headline tax rates and, for this reason, you will not generally see them referred to by the Government or HMRC. But these are the rates that matter for tax planning purposes.

Go back to the dividend tax rates in the table in Chapter 2 (and the notes that follow) and you will see some prime examples of marginal tax rates.

Another prime example of a marginal tax rate is the marginal Corporation Tax rate of 26.5% that we saw in Chapter 2. This rate is going to be very important for small companies making annual profits between £50,000 and £250,000 in the years ahead (or lower levels of profit where the company has any associated companies).

Owing to the transitional rules applying to company accounting periods spanning 1st April 2023, the marginal Corporation Tax rates of companies over the next few years will vary greatly and could be anywhere between 19% and 26.5%.

It is important to understand your company's marginal tax rate as this will determine the value of the Corporation Tax relief you obtain for deductible expenditure or other forms of tax relief you claim.

Your company's marginal tax rate will depend on:

- Its profit level,
- Its accounting period, and
- Whether it has any associated companies

Most companies will see an increase in their marginal Corporation Tax rate over the next few years, thus increasing the value of tax deductible expenditure and tax reliefs.

Example
Timdal Ltd makes annual profits in the range £150,000 to £200,000. It draws up accounts to 31st December each year and has no associated companies. Its marginal Corporation Tax rates over the next few years will be as follows:

Year ending 31st December 2022:	*19.00%*
Year ending 31st December 2023:	*24.65%*
Year ending 31st December 2024:	*26.50%*

This means £10,000 of deductible expenditure will result in tax savings of £1,900 if incurred in 2022; £2,465 if incurred in 2023; and £2,650 if incurred in 2024.

As we can see, the general principle for most companies over the next few years is going to be that deferring tax deductible expenditure will lead to greater tax savings. The major exception to this will be small companies with annual profits of £50,000 or less and no associated companies.

Appendix B provides further details of marginal Corporation Tax rates for companies with various accounting periods and profit levels. For a full analysis of how to calculate marginal Corporation Tax rates and the issue of whether companies are associated, see the Taxcafe.co.uk guide *'The Company Tax Changes'*.

In the case of capital expenditure, there are other factors to consider in addition to marginal Corporation Tax rates. We will look at these in Chapter 11.

Future Tax Changes

When carrying out long-term tax planning, it is important to be aware that there may (in fact, probably will) be further tax changes in the future, particularly after the next General Election (likely to be in 2024; but after we had three in the space of four years, who knows?)

Immediate threats of increases in Capital Gains Tax and Inheritance Tax appear to have gone away for the time being, although there is a general feeling that business asset disposal relief's days are numbered, so those who are thinking of 'selling up' might be wise to do so sooner rather than later. Business asset disposal relief could provide a Capital Gains Tax saving of up to £100,000 on a sale of qualifying company shares, or £200,000 for a couple owning a company together.

Cuts in tax relief for pension contributions always seem to be a perennial concern too, although little has yet materialised beyond some tinkering at the periphery.

More generally though, we cannot be certain that further tax increases for small companies and their directors do not lie ahead after 2024. In fact, given the lies they have spun to date, we cannot even be certain the current Government has already done their worst. Small company owners should bear all this in mind when they carry out their tax planning.

Chapter 4

Profit Extraction

Most small company owners need at least some of their company's annual profits to live on. Many also wish to take money out of their company to invest elsewhere, such as in pensions, property, or other business ventures. We all know it is wise not to have all your eggs in one basket.

We refer to taking money out of your own company as 'profit extraction' and doing it as tax efficiently as possible is a key element of tax planning for small companies and their directors. In this chapter and the next, we will look at how the tax changes we saw in Chapter 2 affect this important area of tax planning. For a more thorough and detailed examination of the topic, see the Taxcafe.co.uk guide *'Salary versus Dividends'*.

There are many ways to take money out of your company. While there are others we will consider later, in Chapter 5, the main ones are, of course, salary or dividends and we will look at these in this chapter. However, before that, I would like to give you some guiding principles to consider.

Regardless of whether you want, or need, the cash, you should generally take any income out of your company that creates an overall net tax saving. At present, this can only occur where you have little or no taxable income from outside the company, but the Corporation Tax changes coming in the next couple of years mean this will happen more often in future.

Provided the company has sufficient distributable profits, it's also generally worth taking a dividend at least equal to your available dividend allowance, as this is tax free. Where your other income is less than the personal allowance, it's worth increasing this by any further tax-free amounts. For example, if your only other income is a salary of £9,568, you can take a total tax free dividend of £5,002 (your personal allowance of £12,570 plus your dividend allowance of £2,000, less the salary).

Arguably, you should also take out anything with a low overall net tax cost, as it may be cheaper than anything available to you in the future. We'll look at this idea further in Chapter 6.

Where these strategies result in you extracting more funds than you actually want, or need, you can lend the surplus back to your company. You'll then be able to withdraw those funds at a later date, tax free (since you will simply be receiving a loan repayment).

Salary

Salary has the advantage that provided the amount being paid is justified by the work the recipient does for the company, it attracts Corporation Tax relief. In this respect, the small, tax-efficient salaries taken by most small company owners are easily justified. Furthermore, in most small companies, I have always taken the view that, if the profits are there in the company, it must be down to the owner/director's efforts that those profits exist: hence any salary or other remuneration paid to them out of those profits must be justified. 'QED' as my old maths teacher would have said.

So, in short, we can generally say directors' salaries will attract Corporation Tax relief. With Corporation Tax rates increasing, this will make paying salaries more worthwhile.

However, the disadvantage of salaries is that they attract Income Tax at higher rates than dividends and are also subject to both employer's and employee's National Insurance, including the Health and Social Care Levy when it arrives in April 2023. Hence, subject to the exemptions and reliefs we looked at in Chapter 2, the National Insurance increase will make salaries above the secondary National Insurance threshold (£9,100 for 2022/23) 1.25% more costly and salaries above the primary threshold (£9,880 for 2022/23) 2.5% more costly.

So the position for director's salaries is changing significantly, but with conflicting factors to consider. Before we look at what this all means for tax-efficient profit extraction in the future, we need to look at the main alternative.

Dividends

Dividends have the advantage that they are subject to lower rates of Income Tax than other forms of taxable income and are exempt from National Insurance. However, as we know, the rates of Income Tax on dividends are to increase by 1.25% from 6th April 2022, mirroring the National Insurance increase. Hence, in effect, from the individual recipient's point of view, the differential in the personal tax cost between dividends and salary will broadly remain the same, although with a few exceptions to consider.

The disadvantage of dividends is they do not attract Corporation Tax relief, as they must be paid out of after tax profits. Hence, broadly speaking, the increase in the Corporation Tax rate will make dividends less attractive by comparison with other forms of profit extraction. Against this we must weigh the fact that, while dividends will suffer the same 1.25% tax increase as salaries from the recipient's point of view, the company will not suffer the further 1.25% cost increase that will apply to salaries above the secondary National Insurance threshold.

The Changing Face of Salary versus Dividends

Sticking for the moment with our two main forms of profit extraction, the position in future will, as ever, depend on how much other taxable income the owner/director receives from outside the company, and what type.

Achieving the optimum profit extraction strategy can sometimes by a highly complex issue and is examined in depth in the Taxcafe.co.uk guide *'Salary versus Dividends'*. Nonetheless, the current position can easily be summed up by saying that, in most cases, owner/directors should first tax a small salary and then take the remainder of any profits they wish to extract by way of dividend.

The question is how much salary should you take, and how much will this be affected by the tax changes we looked at in Chapter 2?

One of the main factors that will determine your ideal salary level is the issue of whether the employment allowance is available. We looked at the general rules governing the employment allowance in Chapter 2.

In Chapter 7, we will look at how far the employment allowance can go and we will see it will not stretch as far in 2022/23 as it does at present, in 2021/22. How far it will stretch in 2023/24 is currently unclear, as we do not yet know whether it will cover the Health and Social Care Levy.

Note that, for the remainder of this chapter and Chapter 5, we will assume the owner/director has already taken out a dividend equal to their available dividend allowance, as this will nearly always be a sensible thing to do. All further references to dividends refer to dividends not covered by the dividend allowance and thus subject to an Income Tax charge. This will reflect the reality of the position in most cases, but it remains important to remember that any payments which create an overall net tax saving should be prioritised even before the dividend allowance.

No Other Income: General

In the current 2021/22 tax year, the most tax efficient level of salary for many owner/directors with no other taxable income is £9,568, equal to the National Insurance primary threshold. Where the employment allowance is not available, this gives rise to a small cost in employer's National Insurance of £100, but is otherwise tax free.

The salary and related National Insurance are eligible for Corporation Tax relief, saving the company £1,837 in Corporation Tax at the current rate of 19%. Hence, overall, the salary provides a net *saving* of £1,737.

In 2022/23, the same strategy will mean paying a salary of £9,880. The National Insurance cost will increase to £117 but will still be far outweighed by the Corporation Tax saving the salary creates. That saving will be at least £1,899, but will be more in many cases.

And it will remain the same in future years. This small salary, equal to the National Insurance primary threshold will always be worthwhile. Yes, a small part of it will attract both employer's National Insurance and the Health and Social Care Levy at a total of 15.05%, but this is outweighed by Corporation Tax relief at a rate of at least 19%.

No Other Income: Special Cases

Currently, where **either** the employment allowance is available (see Chapters 2 and 7 for details) **or** the director is over state pension age, it is worth increasing their salary to £12,570, the level of the personal allowance.

This is because the salary will be free of Income Tax and will only attract one kind of National Insurance (there is no employee's National Insurance where the director is over state pension age, and no employer's National Insurance where the employment allowance is available). Hence the tax cost on part of the salary is either 12% or 13.8% and the Corporation Tax relief is greater, at 19%.

The same principle will apply in future years. The tax cost on part of the salary where the employment allowance is available will be 13.25% for the employee and a maximum of 1.25% for the employer, a total of 14.5%. (Remember, we do not know whether the employment allowance will cover the Health and Social Care Levy from 2023/24 onwards.)

The tax cost on part of the salary where the director is over state pension age will be 1.25% for the employee and 15.05% for the employer, a total of 16.3%.

Since Corporation Tax relief will be available at a rate of at least 19%, possibly more, the same strategy remains worthwhile in both cases.

Where the director is over state pension age **and** the employment allowance is available, even higher salary levels may be worthwhile, but this becomes a complex area.

Some Other Income

Where the director has a small amount of other income from outside the company, the above strategies generally remain sound but may need to be adapted slightly.

If the other income is interest of no more than £500 and/or dividends of no more than £2,000, the same salary levels will generally remain beneficial.

In other cases, the position can get quite complicated but it will always be worth paying any salary that is not subject to Income Tax (i.e. it is covered by the director's personal allowance) and which is subject to either no National Insurance, or only one type of National Insurance (i.e. either employer's or employee's, but not both).

These principles will not change next year when the National Insurance rates increase, nor the year after when the Health and Social Care Levy is introduced. Where there is only one type of National Insurance and no Income Tax, the maximum cost, even taking the Health and Social Care Levy into account, will be 16.3% (as we saw above) and will always be less than Corporation Tax relief at a rate of at least 19%.

However, the position changes once the director's personal allowance has been fully utilised and the salary begins to attract Income Tax.

Basic Rate Taxpayers

So far, we've looked at salaries that create an overall net tax saving and hence are always worthwhile. As we have seen, these arise where the salary is covered by the director's personal allowance and is subject to either no National Insurance, or only one type of National Insurance. We have also seen that the future tax changes examined in Chapter 2 will not alter this principle even taking the Health and Social Care Levy into account from 2023/24 onwards.

At present, once the director's personal allowance has been fully utilised, any salary will give rise to an overall tax cost. Even if there is no National Insurance, the Income Tax arising at 20% will be greater than Corporation Tax relief at 19%.

But that overall cost of 1% is better than the 7.5% basic rate taxpayers currently suffer on dividends, so a salary equal to the National Insurance secondary threshold of £8,840 is still generally a good idea.

That optimal salary increases to £9,568 where the employment allowance is available: generally more where the director is also over state pension age.

Next year (2022/23), Income Tax rates on salaries will remain the same but many companies will begin to see their marginal Corporation Tax rate increase. In many cases this will mean a salary of £9,100 (next year's National Insurance secondary threshold) paid to a basic rate taxpayer director will produce an overall net saving. This net saving arises when the company's marginal Corporation Tax rate increases above 20% and Appendix B will show you whether this applies to your company.

Again, the tax saving salary increases to the level of the National Insurance primary threshold (£9,880 for 2022/23) where the employment allowance is available: generally more where the director is also over state pension age.

At a marginal Corporation Tax rate of 20% or less, the same levels of salary will not produce an overall net saving, but will still be preferable to dividends.

Once National Insurance begins to arise, the current overall net tax cost of any further salary in 2021/22 exceeds the Income Tax payable on a dividend. Hence, dividends generally become preferable for a basic rate taxpayer when a salary would attract either type of National Insurance. However, next year, this position will change in some cases.

Where the salary attracts employer's National Insurance, but not employee's National Insurance, it will be preferable to a dividend where the company's marginal Corporation Tax rate is at least 23.8% (see Appendix B). This will arise on salaries up to the National Insurance primary threshold of £9,880 and any level of salary paid to a basic rate taxpayer over state pension age.

Example
Piebro Ltd is anticipating a profit of around £125,000 for the year ending 31st December 2023, meaning it will have a marginal Corporation Tax rate of 24.651% (see Appendix B). It has a number of employees and has fully utilised its employment allowance for 2022/23.

The Company's owner, Judi, is aged 70. In the tax year 2022/23, she has pension income of £15,000 and has already taken a salary of £9,100 and dividends of £2,000 out of Piebro Ltd.

In March 2023, Judi needs a further net, after tax, sum of £10,000 and is trying to decide whether to take it by way of salary or dividend.

If Judi takes a further dividend of £10,959, she will suffer Income Tax at 8.75%, or £959, leaving her with the required £10,000. So, that's a tax cost of £959.

If Judi takes a further salary of £12,500, she will suffer Income Tax at 20%, or £2,500, and will again be left with the required £10,000. The company will have to pay National Insurance at 15.05%, or £1,881, but will obtain Corporation Tax relief at 24.651% on its total cost of £14,381, providing a saving of £3,545.

The overall net tax cost of the salary is thus £836 (£2,500 + £1,881 – £3,545), meaning it is the better option in this case.

Readers may wonder how this arises when Income Tax at 20% plus employer's National Insurance at 15.05% less Corporation Tax relief at 24.65% appears to equate to 10.4%, which is more than the 8.75% in Income Tax that Judi would have paid on a dividend. However, what tips the balance is the Corporation Tax relief for the employer's National Insurance, which reduces the effective, after tax cost of the National Insurance to 11.34% in this case. Since 20% plus 11.34% minus 24.65% equals less than 8.75%, a saving is produced.

Where the salary attracts employee's National Insurance, it can never be preferable to a dividend for a basic rate taxpayer, even when the employment allowance is available. Don't believe me? I'll show you.

Example
Dancra Ltd draws up accounts to 31ˢᵗ March each year and generally makes a profit of around £200,000. This means, in the year ending 31ˢᵗ March 2024, the company faces the highest possible marginal Corporation Tax rate: 26.5%.

During 2022/23, the company's two directors, Naomie and Ben, have each received rental profits of £10,000 from outside the company, in addition to taking salaries of £9,880 and dividends of £2,000 from Dancra Ltd.

On 3ʳᵈ April 2023, Naomie is reviewing the company's accounts and decides there is a further £18,000 available for the couple to take out. If they take it as additional salary, it will attract Corporation Tax relief at 26.5%, meaning they can actually take out £24,490.

The company has no other employees, so there will be no employer's National Insurance, thanks to the employment allowance.

However, Naomie and Ben will both suffer Income Tax at 20% and employee's National Insurance at 13.25%, leaving them with just £16,347 after tax.

Alternatively, if the company pays dividends of £18,000, the couple will suffer Income Tax at just 8.75% and will be left with £16,425.

As we can see, even at the highest marginal Corporation Tax rate, and with the employment allowance available, dividends are preferable for basic rate taxpayers where a salary would be subject to employee's National Insurance.

In the following year, 2023/24, the position will generally be the same, although marginal Corporation Tax rates will be higher for many companies, meaning the points made above become even more relevant.

Nonetheless, the rebranding of the National Insurance increase as the Health and Social Care Levy will create some new scenarios to consider.

Firstly, we do not yet know whether the employment allowance will be available to cover the employer's element of the Health and Social Care Levy. If it *is* then the position for owner/directors under state pension age will be the same in 2023/24 as in 2022/23.

If the employment allowance does ***not*** cover the Health and Social Care Levy, it will still be worth paying salaries up to the National Insurance primary threshold where the allowance is available to cover the employer's National Insurance. Where the company's marginal Corporation Tax rate is at least 21%, the increase in salary from the National Insurance secondary threshold to the primary threshold produces a further overall net tax saving; although this level of salary is still preferable to dividends at any Corporation Tax rate.

Where the employment allowance is not available, paying salaries up to the National Insurance primary threshold will again be preferable to dividends when the company's marginal Corporation Tax rate is at least 23.8% (see Appendix B).

The second important change in 2023/24 will only affect directors over state pension age. While these directors will continue to be exempt from employee's National Insurance, they will be subject to the Health and Social Care Levy. However, despite this, salaries paid to basic rate taxpayers over state pension age in 2023/24 will:

- Be preferable to dividends where the company's marginal Corporation Tax rate is 25% or more
- Be preferable to dividends where the employment allowance is available
- Produce an overall net tax saving where the company's marginal Corporation Tax rate is at least 22.25% and the employment allowance is available to cover employer's National Insurance only
- Produce an overall net tax saving where the company's marginal Corporation Tax rate is at least 21.25% and the employment allowance is available to cover both employer's National Insurance and the Health and Social Care Levy

Higher Rate Taxpayers

A salary paid to a director who is already a higher rate taxpayer can never produce an overall net tax saving. However, the question remains as to whether such salaries should be paid before dividends.

For salaries up to the National Insurance secondary threshold, the answer is yes, regardless of the tax year concerned or the company's marginal Corporation Tax rate, as these will always have a lower overall net tax cost than dividends.

Where the employment allowance is available, a salary up to the National Insurance primary threshold is preferable to dividends. This will remain the case in both 2022/23 and 2023/24 even if the employment allowance does not cover the Health and Social Care Levy.

Beyond this, it will generally be preferable for higher rate taxpayer directors to take any further amounts by way of dividend.

However, there are exceptions, including directors:

- With substantial employment income from other sources outside the company
- With substantial partnership or self-employment trading income in addition to the income from their company
- Over state pension age

The first two groups are too complex for the scope of this guide but are covered in the Taxcafe.co.uk guide *'Salary versus Dividends'*.

As far as higher rate taxpayer directors over state pension age are concerned, additional salary is only preferable in the current 2021/22 tax year where the employment allowance is available.

In both 2022/23 and 2023/24, additional salary will continue to be preferable to dividends for higher rate taxpayer directors over state pension age where the employment allowance is available (even if the allowance does not cover the Health and Social Care Levy).

In 2022/23, additional salary will also be better for these directors where the company's marginal Corporation Tax rate is at least 21.3% (see Appendix B).

In 2023/24, additional salary will also be better for these directors where the company's marginal Corporation Tax rate is at least 23% (see Appendix B).

The position for additional rate taxpayers with taxable income in excess of £150,000 is generally the same as for higher rate taxpayers.

However, the position may sometimes differ slightly from the analysis above where the director's taxable income is in the bracket from £100,000 to £125,140 and further payments lead to the loss of some or all of their personal allowance.

Chapter 5

Other Ways to Get Money Out of Your Company

As we have seen, dividends have the disadvantage that they do not attract Corporation Tax relief and, subject to the points made in Chapter 4, salaries generally carry the problem of being subject to National Insurance.

Hence, any form of profit extraction that attracts Corporation Tax relief but does not give rise to National Insurance is potentially preferable to both salaries and dividends. Payments falling into this category include interest, rent, and pension contributions.

Interest

Where the director has loaned money to the company, they can charge interest at anything up to a reasonable arms' length commercial rate and this will attract Corporation Tax relief. Basic rate Income Tax at 20% must be deducted from payments to the director but can be set off against other tax liabilities or, if appropriate, recovered, when the director submits their self-assessment tax return.

Interest is tax-free when it is covered by the personal allowance, the starting rate band, or the personal savings allowance. This allows many directors to receive up to £18,570 in tax free interest, or £9,730 if they are also taking a salary of £8,840 (the current National Insurance secondary threshold).

This tax-free sum of up to £18,570 will remain unchanged in future years, but the Corporation Tax relief it provides will increase in value, in most cases, as the company's marginal Corporation Tax rate increases.

If the company's marginal Corporation Tax rate increases to more than 20%, further interest payments, while subject to Income Tax, will still give rise to an overall net tax saving on payments up to a potential maximum of £50,270 per year.

Even beyond this, interest payments are more tax efficient than dividends, or salaries subject to National Insurance or the Health and Social Care Levy.

Rent

Directors can charge rent on property or other assets they own personally but which are used by their company. Provided the rent charged does not exceed an arms' length commercial rate, the payments will attract Corporation Tax relief.

Future increases in marginal Corporation Tax rates will make this strategy even more worthwhile. Many companies will see their marginal Corporation Tax rate increase to more than 20%, meaning rent of up to £50,270 per year will give rise to an overall net tax saving.

Even beyond this, rent remains more tax efficient than dividends, or salaries subject to National Insurance or the Health and Social Care Levy.

However, owning property personally and renting it to your company carries some potential long-term disadvantages. Charging rent may affect any future business asset disposal relief claim for Capital Gains Tax purposes, although this will often be of no concern since there is now a £1m lifetime limit on gains subject to this relief (for further details, see the Taxcafe.co.uk guide *'How to Save Property Tax'*).

Perhaps more importantly, owning business property personally may reduce the property's potential Inheritance Tax exemption from 100% to just 50% (for further details, see the Taxcafe.co.uk guide *'How to Save Inheritance Tax'*).

Pension Contributions

Pensions have something of a 'marmite' character: you either love them or you hate them (or at least distrust them, anyway). In over thirty years of advising small company owners, I met some who wanted to put as much in their pension fund as possible and some who avoided pensions like the plague. They all had their reasons and, at the end of the day, whether to trust your money to a pension scheme is very much a personal choice. Nonetheless it must be said that pension savings are generally very tax-efficient.

As with salary, a pension contribution made by the company on behalf of a director will attract Corporation Tax relief provided the contribution is justified by the work the director does for the company. (See my comments in Chapter 4 under 'Salary'.)

Provided you stick within the appropriate limits, company pension contributions are free from National Insurance and will not give rise to any Income Tax charges at the point of payment.

Your company can generally make a maximum contribution of £40,000 per year on your behalf. This can be 'rolled up' for up to four years in many cases, but there are also further restrictions to be considered.

The main disadvantage of pension contributions for younger directors is that the funds are effectively locked away until they reach the age of 55 (rising to 57 from 2028).

However, subject to this, company pension contributions will become more attractive in the coming years, as many companies see their marginal Corporation Tax rates increasing. Furthermore, while Income Tax will arise on future withdrawals (apart from an initial 25% tax-free lump sum), pension income is exempt from National Insurance, and will also be exempt from the Health and Social Care Levy.

Example
Davniv Ltd makes annual profits of around £230,000. It has a number of employees and always uses its employment allowance. The company's owner/director, Peter, was born in 1968. He is in a pension scheme, but has only made one nominal contribution, five years ago. He takes a salary from Davniv Ltd equal to the National Insurance primary threshold each year and always uses his dividend allowance. He also has rental income of £6,000 per year, making him a basic rate taxpayer.

During the year ending 31ˢᵗ March 2024, Davniv Ltd makes a contribution of £160,000 to Peter's pension scheme. The contribution provides Corporation Tax relief at an effective rate of 26.5%, saving the company £42,400.

In 2024/25, Peter withdraws the tax-free lump sum of £40,000 from his pension fund. In each year from 2025/26 to 2028/29 he withdraws a further £30,000. The total Income Tax paid by Peter on his withdrawals is £24,000.

*If we take the company's Corporation Tax relief into account, there is an overall net tax **saving** of £18,400, while at the same time, a net sum of £136,000 has been put into Peter's hands.*

To put this same net sum into Peter's hands over the same period would have cost £13,041 in Income Tax if paid by way of dividend. The overall net tax cost of paying it by way of salary would have been £36,291.

For the sake of illustration, I have ignored the tax-free growth of the funds within Peter's pension scheme (another tax advantage) between the time of the company's contribution and the later withdrawals. I have also ignored the value of his earlier nominal contribution.

For further details of the benefits, and limitations, of pension contributions, see the Taxcafe.co.uk guide *'Pension Magic'*.

Benefits-in-Kind

In Chapter 7, we will look at some of the benefits-in-kind that could be used to reduce the cost of employment. In many cases, the same benefits could be used as another means for owner/directors to effectively extract funds from their company tax efficiently.

A tax-free benefit will provide Corporation Tax relief (subject to the usual provision regarding the director's total remuneration being justified) and thus an overall net tax saving of between 19% and 26.5%.

A benefit that is subject to Income Tax and employer's National Insurance but which is exempt from employee's National Insurance and also provides Corporation Tax relief will:

- Produce an overall net tax saving where the director has not fully utilised their Income Tax personal allowance
- Have a lower overall net tax cost than most salaries in excess of the National Insurance primary threshold (except salaries paid to directors over state pension age before 6th April 2023)

- Have a lower overall net tax cost than dividends where the director is a basic rate taxpayer and the company's marginal Corporation Tax rate is at least 23.8% (see Appendix B)
- Have a lower overall net tax cost than dividends where the director is a higher or additional rate taxpayer and the company's marginal Corporation Tax rate is at least 21.3% (see Appendix B)

Paying Family Members

Spreading the company's ownership around the family will generally help to reduce the tax costs of profit extraction. For example, a couple and three adult children owning shares in a family company may be able to take a total of up to £72,850 in tax free dividends each year (less if any of them have other sources of income).

However, this is not suitable for everyone since:

- Transfers of shares to anyone other than your spouse may give rise to Capital Gains Tax liabilities
- Each shareholder must have beneficial entitlement to the shares, any income derived from them, and any sale proceeds
- Minor children cannot hold shares directly. Shares can be placed in trust for their benefit but this has many complex tax implications and, if the shares are provided by the children's parents, the income derived from them is taxed on the parents. For further information, see the Taxcafe.co.uk guide 'How to Save Inheritance Tax'.

Another way to reduce the cost of profit extraction is to pay salaries to family members. Children only need to be at least 13 or 14 (depending on the local authority) and salaries paid to those under 16 are exempt from all classes of National Insurance (it seems likely these will also be exempt from the Health and Social Care Levy). However, payments made to any family member must be justified by the work they do for the company and there are restrictions on the hours and type of work children under school leaving age are allowed to do.

Nonetheless, paying your children tax-deductible wages is a great deal better than giving them pocket money out of your own after tax income.

With the forthcoming increases in both Income Tax on dividends and Corporation Tax rates, this strategy will save even more in future.

Example

Ian is a higher rate taxpayer. He owns Barnel Ltd, which makes annual profits of around £150,000 and draws up accounts to 31st March each year.

Ian has three children: Jimmy, born in July 2003, and currently at university; Vesper, born in 2005, and currently at sixth form college studying for her 'A' levels; and Felix, born in 2008, who is still at school.

Previously, Ian was giving £125 per week to Jimmy to help with rent and food, pocket money of £50 per week to Vesper, and £30 per week to Felix. This totalled £205 per week, or £10,660 per year. To fund this expenditure, Ian had to take additional dividends of £15,793 out of Barnel Ltd, which cost him £5,133 in Income Tax (£15,793 less £5,133 in tax left the net sum of £10,660 Ian needed).

If he carried on the same way in 2022/23, the cost would increase to £5,431 because of the increase in Income Tax rates on dividends.

Instead, Ian offers to pay each of the children 50% more if they work at Barnel Ltd during their holidays. They all go for it and the total wages he pays to them amount to £15,990. This saves the company £3,038 in Corporation Tax (at 19%) and also means Ian saves £5,431 in Income Tax, a total saving of £8,469, which more than covers the extra £5,330 paid to the children.

There is no National Insurance on the children's wages since they all earn less than the National Insurance primary threshold and are all aged under 21.

The following year, 2023/24, the company's saving, at a marginal Corporation Tax rate of 26.5% increases to £4,237, giving rise to a total saving of £9,668.

In summary, this strategy has produced three major benefits:

- Tax savings totalling £9,668
- The children are all 50% better off
- Ian has got his children to do some work for his company

That last one may seem a little 'tongue in cheek' but not only is it saving tax now, it may help with succession planning in the future.

Borrowing from Your Company

There are no longer any legal restrictions on a director borrowing from their own company, provided the company remains solvent. However, borrowing from your company can potentially result in several tax charges.

Firstly, a Corporation Tax charge (known as the 'Section 455 charge') of 32.5% on any amounts still outstanding nine months after the company's accounting date. This charge will increase to 33.75% for amounts borrowed after 5th April 2022. The Section 455 tax is repayable when the loan itself has been repaid, but there can be a considerable delay in some cases.

Secondly, the director is subject to an Income Tax benefit-in-kind charge on any deemed beneficial loan interest. This is the amount by which any interest actually paid to the company by the director on their loan is less than interest at the 'official rate', which is currently just 2% (although it seems likely to increase back to 2.25%, its previous level, from 6th April 2022). However, where the director's total indebtedness to the company never exceeds £10,000 throughout the tax year, there is no benefit-in-kind charge.

Thirdly, any benefit-in-kind charge that arises is subject to employer's National Insurance. This will include the increased rate applying in 2022/23 and the Health and Social Care Levy from 2023/24 onwards.

Income Tax and National Insurance can be avoided if the director pays interest to the company at the official rate. While this leads to a Corporation Tax cost on this income, it will generally be cheaper overall.

Armed with the knowledge of these rules, it is possible to use loans as a cheaper form of profit extraction than dividends.

Example

Holly is a higher rate taxpayer. In March 2022, she needs to extract a net, after tax, sum of £10,000 from her company, Bobhol Ltd. To get this amount after tax, she would need to take a dividend of £14,815. This would cost her £4,815 in Income Tax (at 32.5%), leaving the required net sum.

Alternatively, if she borrows £10,000 from Bobhol Ltd, and does not repay the money within nine months after the end of the company's accounting period, there will be a Section 455 charge of £3,250 (again, at 32.5%).

As we can readily see, because the Section 455 tax is paid by the company and not by the director, there is no effective grossing up, as there would be for a dividend. Hence, taking the money by way of loan would save £1,565 in tax, or 15.65% of the amount borrowed.

In other words, although the tax rates on both the dividend and the loan appear to be the same, in practice they're not, and loans can often provide a cheaper alternative.

Both tax rates will go up to 33.75% from 6th April 2022, but the principles will remain the same. If Holly were in the same position after that date, a dividend would cost her £5,094 if she needed a net, after tax sum of £10,000, whereas a loan would only cost £3,375. The saving arising will thus increase to £1,719, or 17.19%.

This strategy is not a good idea for basic rate taxpayers, but is even more beneficial for additional rate taxpayers, as Section 455 tax is charged at the same rate regardless of the director's personal tax position. As a result, additional rate taxpayers currently save 29.05% by taking a loan instead of a dividend, increasing to 31.13% from 6th April 2022.

These savings will be slightly reduced if the director borrows more than £10,000 and is either subject to a benefit-in-kind charge or must pay interest to the company which, in turn, will be subject to Corporation Tax. Even so, the strategy will often remain worthwhile.

Example

Kissy has no sources of income other than her company, Micjay Ltd. During the 2021/22 tax year, she has taken a salary of £9,568 and dividends of £88,000, meaning her taxable income totals £97,568 and more than £2,432 of further income will result in the withdrawal of her personal allowance.

She now wishes to extract a further net, after tax, sum of £25,000 from Micjay Ltd. Due to the impact on her personal allowance, to do this by way of dividend will mean taking out a sum of £44,861 and paying additional Income Tax of £19,861.

Instead, Kissy borrows £25,000 from Micjay Ltd, resulting in a Section 455 charge, at 32.5%, of £8,125, a saving of £11,736 compared with the cost of a dividend.

At this point, we can see another advantage of borrowing from your company: as borrowings are not classed as taxable income, they cannot lead to the withdrawal of the owner/director's personal allowance.

Let's assume Kissy borrowed the money from Micjay Ltd on 1st April 2022 and the company has a 31st March accounting date. Let's also assume (as seems likely) that the official rate of interest increases back to 2.25% from 6th April 2022.

Example Continued

Kissy agrees to pay Micjay Ltd interest at 2.25% on her loan. This amounts to £562 per year. For the year ending 31st March 2023, the company will suffer Corporation Tax at 19% on this additional income, or the grand sum of £107. Kissy takes an extra dividend of £849 to fund the interest, giving her an additional Income Tax cost of £287. All, in all, the loan leads to a tax cost of £394 in 2022/23.

In 2023/24 the company's marginal Corporation Tax rate will increase to either 25% or 26.5% (given the dividends it is paying, it must be making profits of more than £50,000). At worst, the additional Corporation Tax on its interest income is thus £149, increasing the annual tax cost of the loan to £436 (£287 + £149).

In summary, taking a loan saved £11,736 compared to the cost of a dividend and, while it gives rise to a small annual tax cost, it will take at least 27 years before that annual cost outweighs the initial saving.

And the tax changes lying ahead will only make this strategy even more worthwhile, if Kissy was in the same position a year later, near the end of the 2022/23 tax year, a dividend would cost her £20,817 in extra Income Tax, whereas a loan would lead to a Section 455 charge of £8,437, meaning the overall saving increases to £12,380 and it will take at least 28 years before the annual cost outweighs that saving.

Furthermore, remember, the Section 455 tax is like a loan to the Government. That loan itself will be repaid when the owner/director repays the loan from the company.

Chapter 6

Pay Now, Save Later

As I mentioned at the start of Chapter 4, it may make sense to take more funds out of the company now than you currently need, if this can be done at a lower overall net tax cost than you are likely to face in the future.

The changes we looked at in Chapter 2 make this idea particularly relevant at the moment. To a large extent, subject to the company's profitability and the director's personal needs, small company owners are able to control the amount of income they take out of their company. This means they can limit their individual taxable income in order to avoid exceeding key thresholds, such as the:

- Child Benefit Charge threshold: £50,000
- Higher rate tax threshold: £50,270
- Point at which their personal allowance begins to be withdrawn: £100,000
- Additional rate tax threshold: £150,000

However, we know the higher rate tax threshold will remain frozen at its current level until April 2026, and the other thresholds have never changed since they were introduced, so they are likely to remain frozen too.

This means, with inflation now on the increase, the real value of these thresholds will reduce. Add to this the increase in dividend tax rates and many owner/directors will find it difficult to maintain their standard of living without moving into a higher tax bracket.

Let's take the example of a small company owner who has no other sources of income and takes a salary equal to the National Insurance primary threshold plus sufficient dividends to bring their total income up to the higher rate tax threshold each year.

Let's add the assumption that inflation will run at 3.5% over the period of the tax threshold freeze. The table below sets out the after tax income the company owner receives in both absolute terms, and in real terms, as adjusted for inflation, to show the equivalent net income in 2021/22.

After Tax Income at Higher Rate Tax Threshold

Year	Absolute Terms	Real Terms
2021/22	£47,593	£47,593
2022/23	£47,146	£45,552
2023/24	£47,146	£44,012
2024/25	£47,146	£42,523
2025/26	£47,146	£41,085

If this company owner needs to restore their lost 'real terms' income, they will need to pay Income Tax at 33.75% on the additional dividends they will need to take. By 2025/26, to get back the lost 'real' income of £6,508 will need further actual after tax income of £7,467 which will mean taking extra dividends of £11,271 and paying extra tax of £3,804.

Looked at another way, to maintain the same after tax income in real terms, this small company owner will be paying £6,928 in Income Tax by 2025/26 compared with £2,678 in 2021/22.

Let's take another example: a small company owner, again with no other sources of income, who takes a salary equal to the National Insurance primary threshold plus sufficient dividends to bring their total income up to £100,000 each year, thus preserving their personal allowance.

Again, the table below sets out the after tax income the company owner receives in both absolute terms, and in real terms, as adjusted for inflation.

After Tax Income at £100,000 of Taxable Income

Year	Absolute Terms	Real Terms
2021/22	£81,160	£81,160
2022/23	£80,092	£77,384
2023/24	£80,092	£74,767
2024/25	£80,092	£72,239
2025/26	£80,092	£69,796

By 2025/26, this company owner has lost £11,364 of income in 'real terms'. To restore it, they will need to both suffer Income Tax at 33.75% on the additional dividends they need to take and suffer the loss of their personal allowance.

In fact, to restore their position in real terms, they will need further actual after tax income of £13,041, which will mean taking extra dividends of £27,951 and paying extra tax of £14,910.

(Due to the impact of the lost personal allowance, this is a complex calculation, partly affected by the level of the National Insurance primary threshold in 2025/26, which I have assumed to be £10,972, based on annual inflation at 3.5%)

Looked at another way, to maintain the same after tax income in real terms, this small company owner will be paying £34,818 in Income Tax by 2025/26 compared with £18,840 in 2021/22.

These dramatic increases in tax bills for those simply trying to maintain the same level of income in real terms demonstrate the impact of being pushed into a higher tax bracket in the future: a likely outcome for many small company owners over the period of the big freeze in Income Tax thresholds.

One way to combat this is to utilise any opportunities to take lower cost income out of your company now. It will often make sense to pay a little more now, in order to save a lot more later on. The example that follows may get a little complex (tax is complex), but it will prove the point admirably.

Example
Miranda and Gustav are the owner/directors of Tobstep Ltd. They want to build the company up, so they only take out the money they need. They have four young children, so their living costs are quite high. Nonetheless, at present, they can get by on £7,500 a month, or £90,000 a year. They receive £3,284 in child benefit for 2021/22, meaning they need a net, after tax, sum of £86,716 out of Tobstep Ltd.

They can get this by each taking a salary of £9,568 and dividends of £36,124, giving them total taxable income of £45,692 each and thus ensuring they remain basic rate taxpayers and are not subject to the Child Benefit Charge. In fact, their total tax bill is just £4,668 and their marginal tax rate is 7.5%.

In 2022/23, the couple's child benefit increases to £3,388 but with real inflation (per the RPI) running at, say, 5%, their living costs increase to £94,500, meaning they need to take a net, after tax, sum of £91,112 out of Tobstep Ltd. This is going to entail taking a larger dividend in addition to the salaries of £9,880 they will each be able to take, and this will be exacerbated by the increase in dividend tax rates. In fact, Miranda and Gustav will each need to take a dividend of £38,647, giving them total taxable income of £48,527 each, which is getting perilously close to both the Child Benefit Charge threshold and the higher rate tax threshold.

Their total tax bill is now £5,942 and their marginal tax rate is 8.75%.

In 2023/24, let's assume both child benefit and the National Insurance primary threshold are increased in line with CPI inflation at 3.5% but Miranda and Gustav's living costs again increase by 5%, to £99,225. They will receive £3,507 in child benefit, meaning they need a net, after tax, sum of £95,718 from Tobstep Ltd.

Based on our assumptions, they would be able to take salaries of £10,244 each and would need to take dividends of £41,578 each. This gives them taxable income of £51,822 each and costs the following in Income Tax:

£35,700* x 8.75% =	£3,124 each x 2 =	£6,248
£1,552** x 33.75% =	£524 each x 2 =	£1,048
Child Benefit Charge (18%***)		£631
Total		£7,927

* Basic rate band less dividend allowance
** Income in excess of higher rate tax threshold
*** 1% of child benefit claimed for each £100 in income above £50,000 (for the highest earner in the household)

As we can see, there has been a significant increase in the couple's total tax bill (on top of the additional Corporation Tax Tobstep Ltd will be paying at this point). More importantly, the marginal tax rate on the top £3,104 of the couple's income (£1,552 each) is a whopping 51.3%. This comprises dividend tax at 33.75% plus the Child Benefit Charge, which actually works out at 35.07%, but is only charged on one of the couple, so it averages out at just over 17.5%.

And this is just the beginning, if we follow all the same assumptions for 2024/25, Miranda and Gustav will receive £3,630 in child benefit, but their living costs will have reached £104,186, so they will need net, after tax, income of £100,556 from Tobstep Ltd, requiring salaries of £10,608 each and dividends of £46,252 each.

This gives them taxable income of £56,860 each and costs the following in Income Tax:

£35,700 x 8.75% =	*£3,124 each x 2 =*	*£6,248*
£6,590 x 33.75% =	*£2,224 each x 2 =*	*£4,448*
Child Benefit Charge (68%)		*£2,468*
Total		*£13,164*

Not so long ago, they were paying just £4,668 to have the same net income in real terms.

Getting a Head Start

There's a line in one of my favourite songs, 'You can't run away forever, but there's nothing working with getting a good head start'. That's precisely what Miranda and Gustav could have done and it would have saved them a lot of tax.

In 2021/22, each of them could have taken £4,308 in additional dividends without hitting the Child Benefit Charge threshold. The extra Income Tax, at just 7.5%, would have totalled just £646, leaving a net sum of £7,970 which they could have lent back to Tobstep Ltd.

In 2022/23, they could have taken a further £1,473 each, paid Income Tax at 8.75%, a total of £258 between them, and lent the net sum of £2,688 back to Tobstep Ltd, making a total loan of £10,658.

In 2023/24, they could then have limited their dividends to £40,026 each, meaning they remained basic rate taxpayers with taxable income of £50,270 each and Income Tax costs as follows:

£35,700 x 8.75% =	£3,124 each x 2 =	£6,248
Child Benefit Charge (2%)		£70
Total		£6,318

This would have saved them £1,609 (£7,927 – £6,318) in Income Tax. Their net, after tax income would have been £94,222: £1,496 less than they needed, but they could have taken this as a loan repayment from the company.

In 2024/25, they could again limit their dividends to the amount that keeps their taxable income at the higher rate tax threshold of £50,270. Their tax position would be much the same except that, based on out assumptions, their Child Benefit Charge would be £2 more. Hence, this would have saved them a further £6,844 (£13,164 – £6,320) in Income Tax.

Their net, after tax, income would be £94,220 so, to top it up to the £100,556 they require, they could withdraw a further £6,336 from their company loan account, leaving a balance of £2,826 (£10,658 – £1,496 – £6,336).

This final balance of £2,826 can be withdrawn in 2025/26 and will reduce the amount of dividends the couple need to take out of the company. As those dividends would be taxed at 33.75%, it will reduce the amount of dividend they need to take by £4,266, saving them a further £1,440 in Income Tax.

In summary, maximising the dividends they are able to take at lower tax rates of 7.5% in 2021/22 and 8.75% in 2022/23, will cost Miranda and Gustav an extra £904 (£646 + £258) but will lead to the following savings:

2023/24: £1,609
2024/25: £6,844
2025/26: £1,440

That's a total of £9,893, producing an overall net saving of £8,989, almost a ten-fold return on their initial 'investment'. If you can find better than that, tell me about it!

Chapter 7

Cutting the Cost of Employment

As we saw in Chapter 2, the National Insurance increases in 2022/23 and Health and Social Care Levy in 2023/24 will increase the cost of employment by 2.5% in most cases.

2.5% may not sound like much, but many companies already operate on narrow margins. Furthermore, the employment tax increase comes on top of the Corporation Tax and dividend tax increases, which will hit small companies and their owners respectively.

So it makes sense to look at ways of cutting the cost of employing staff where you can.

The Employment Allowance

The employment allowance covers the first £4,000 of employer's National Insurance each tax year, and will continue to do so next year, in 2022/23. But with the increase in the rate of employer's National Insurance from 13.8% to 15.05%, the allowance won't go as far as it does at the moment.

At present, a single owner/director with one monthly paid employee earning £737 per month (i.e. just over the National Insurance secondary threshold), can pay themselves a salary of £37,822 free of employer's National Insurance. (See Chapter 4 for situations where this will be more beneficial than paying dividends)

Next year, 2022/23, the employee's pay will need to increase to £759 per month in order for the company to continue to qualify for the employment allowance (according to HMRC's interpretation of the rules, anyway). The director will then only be able to pay themselves a salary of £35,670 before the company is subject to employer's National Insurance.

Two directors with no employees subject to employer's National Insurance (see Chapter 2 regarding the applicable exemptions) can take salaries of £23,333 each free from employer's National Insurance in 2021/22. In 2023/24, they will only be able to take salaries of £22,389 each. (Again, see Chapter 4 for situations where this may be beneficial.)

The position for 2023/24 and subsequent years depends on whether the employment allowance covers the Health and Social Care Levy. If it does then the position will be similar to 2022/23; if it does not, it will be similar to 2021/22 but, of course, the Health and Social Care Levy will be payable on salaries over the National Insurance secondary threshold. In either case, the amount that can be paid free of employer's National Insurance will increase slightly, due to inflationary increases in the threshold.

Turning to employees more generally, the amount of pay, per employee, that can be covered by the employment allowance can broadly be calculated as follows:

Employees (1)	2021/22	2022/23	2023/24 (2)	2023/24 (3)
1	£37,826	£35,678	£35,990	£38,398
2	£23,333	£22,389	£22,701	£23,905
3	£18,502	£17,959	£18,271	£19,074
4	£16,086	£15,745	£16,057	£16,658
5	£14,637	£14,416	£14,728	£15,209
10	£11,739	£11,758	£12,070	£12,311
20	£10,289	£10,429	£10,741	£10,861

Notes
1. Number of employees not subject to any exemption from employer's National Insurance
2. Assuming the employment allowance covers the Health and Social Care Levy
3. Assuming the employment allowance does not cover the Health and Social Care Levy
4. I have forecast a small increase in the secondary threshold for 2023/24, to £9,412: based on estimated inflation at 3.5% per the CPI

These changes may not look too bad until you look at them in real terms, as adjusted for inflation. If we assume real inflation, per the RPI, at 5%, the current value of these maximum wages free from employer's National Insurance is as follows (notes as above):

Employees (1)	2021/22	2022/23	2023/24 (2)	2023/24 (3)
1	£37,826	£33,979	£32,644	£34,828
2	£23,333	£21,323	£20,591	£21,682
3	£18,502	£17,104	£16,573	£17,301
4	£16,086	£14,995	£14,564	£15,110
5	£14,637	£13,729	£13,358	£13,795
10	£11,739	£11,198	£10,948	£11,166
20	£10,289	£9,932	£9,742	£9,851

If you go back to Chapter 2 and look at the example of Maud and Adam, you will see the impact this could have on a small company and its owners.

Employing the Right People

The above tables make it clear many small companies that are currently sheltered from the cost of employer's National Insurance by the employment allowance will be facing this additional employment cost in future. And those who are already paying will be paying more.

So it makes sense to consider some of the available exemptions such as employing people:

- Under the age of 21
- Under the age of 25 and in a qualifying apprenticeship
- Who have recently left the armed forces

You might even consider using robots instead. (No, this isn't science fiction; there is a restaurant in Japan that is now using robots for its waiting staff.) Personally, I don't like the idea, I prefer dealing with real people, but I suppose it depends what type of business you have.

Beneficial Benefits

As we know, wages and salaries suffer three taxes: Income Tax, employee's National Insurance, and employer's National Insurance. Two of them are being increased; the other will effectively be increased by the Government's freeze on tax thresholds and allowances. In 2023/24, the Government will add a fourth tax on employment, the Health and Social Care Levy.

A benefit-in-kind that avoids all these taxes may be a better alternative to cash salary. The following are some of the benefits that are exempt from all the taxes:

- Workplace car parking
- Pension contributions and up to £500 of pensions advice
- One mobile phone
- Staff parties (costing up to £150 per head)
- Certain types of childcare
- Relocation costs (up to £8,000)
- Work-related training
- Provision of bicycles and cycling safety equipment
- Long-service awards
- In-house gyms and sports facilities
- Health screening and medical check-ups (one per year)
- Cheap/free canteen meals
- Personal gifts unconnected with work (e.g. wedding gifts)
- Business mileage payments
- Protective clothing and uniforms
- Overnight expenses if away on business
- Equipment for disabled employees (e.g. hearing aids)
- Trivial benefits up to £50

Each of these tax-free benefits is subject to specific rules, especially if provided under a salary sacrifice arrangement (such arrangements are now quite restricted). However, the restrictions on salary sacrifice arrangements do not apply to employer pension contributions, employer-provided pensions advice, employer-supported childcare, or cycle to work schemes.

Where the benefit qualifies for exemption from Income Tax and National Insurance, it should also enjoy exemption from the Health and Social Care Levy.

Broadly speaking, any benefits-in-kind not listed above will generally at least escape employee's National Insurance. With the main rate of employee's National Insurance rising to 13.25% from 6th April 2022, this will often be worth exploring.

For example, providing a basic rate taxpayer employee with a gym membership costing £750 a year will save them almost £100 in 2022/23 compared with the equivalent salary.

Historically, benefits that only avoided employee's National Insurance and not the other taxes did not seem very valuable for higher rate taxpayer employees. However, with the additional rate of employee's National Insurance on salaries over £50,270 increasing to 3.25% from 6th April 2022, this may be worth revisiting.

In all cases, benefits-in-kind will only escape employee's National Insurance if:

- They are not given in place of salary to which the employee still has a contractual right (i.e. it has not been foregone or formally sacrificed).
- The employer contracts directly with the provider. If the employer settles an employee's contractual liability, this will be fully taxable, like additional salary.

Subject to the points made in Chapters 4 and 5 regarding owner/directors and their families, the cost of providing benefits to the company's employees is always an allowable deduction for Corporation Tax purposes.

Practical Measures

Another way to cut the cost of employment is to provide 'intangible' benefits (instead of a payrise), such as increased holiday entitlement, allowing flexitime, or, particularly topical at the moment, allowing employees to work from home.

If you want them in the workplace, make it a more pleasant environment, (e.g. buy new office furniture, or redecorate).

There are many other ways to keep your employees happy. If all else fails, why not just be nice to them?

Chapter 8

Year End Planning: Dividends

Key Date to Take Action by: 5th April 2022

Year end planning for dividends is part of your profit extraction strategy, so it needs to be considered in conjunction with the general guidance in Chapter 4.

However, the first point must be to pay any dividends to yourself, as well as your spouse and other family members, if applicable, that are covered by the dividend allowance. It's tax-free, don't miss your chance.

Further tax-free dividends should also be paid where appropriate. Remember, a dividend is tax free up to the amount of your available dividend allowance PLUS and part of your personal allowance not already used up by other income. For an owner/director with a salary of £9,568 and no other income, their maximum tax free dividend is £5,002.

Using the Basic Rate Band

As we saw in Chapter 6, many company owners may be forced into a higher tax bracket in the future due to the freeze in Income Tax thresholds.

Consider if it is worth paying yourself additional dividends by 5th April 2022 that will fall into your basic rate band and be taxed at just 7.5%.

If this means you can pay less dividends in future that will be taxed at 33.75%, you will be saving 26.25% and, as we saw from the example of Miranda and Gustav in Chapter 6, this could be highly beneficial.

However, if you are likely to remain a basic rate taxpayer, it may not be worth taking extra dividends this year, taxed at 7.5%, just to save 1.25% in the long-term.

Having said that, the proportionate increase in the tax on a dividend received by a basic rate taxpayer after 5th April 2022 amounts to 16.7%; so it could be worth taking some extra dividends early.

Example

Joseph takes a salary equal to the National Insurance primary threshold plus sufficient dividends to give him total net, after tax, income of £25,000, out of his company each year.

In 2021/22 this has given him total taxable income of £25,846, meaning £24,424 of his basic rate band is still available.

If he continues to follow this same strategy, it will cost him £1,000 in Income Tax in each future year.

Alternatively, however, he could take an additional dividend of £24,424 by 5th April 2022. This would give rise to extra Income Tax this year of £1,832, leaving a net sum of £22,592, which he can either put on deposit somewhere or lend back to his company.

In 2022/23, he could then restrict his dividends to the maximum tax-free amount. To get the further £10,430 he needs (£25,000 less his £12,570 personal allowance and his £2,000 dividend allowance), he simply withdraws this from his deposit, thus saving him £1,000 in Income Tax.

He can do the same in 2023/24, with the same saving, and in 2024/25 he'll still have £1,732 of his deposit left, meaning he needs £1,898 less dividend, which will save him a final £166.

Paying an extra £1,832 this year saves Joseph £2,166 over the next three years. It may not seem much, but the net saving of £334 is equivalent to a return of nearly 18.25%. You'd struggle to get that out of a bank these days.

Personally, I'd say this modest saving is worthwhile if it will be realised within two or three years (like Joseph), but not if it will take much longer.

Higher Rate Taxpayers

For higher rate taxpayers, it will not usually be worth taking extra dividends this year simply to avoid the 1.25% increase in the dividend tax rate, as this only represents a proportionate increase of 3.85%, much less than for basic rate taxpayers.

However, there are some exceptions. If you are a higher rate taxpayer this year, but expect to be an additional rate taxpayer next year, it may be worth taking more dividends taxed at 32.5% this year rather than at 39.35% next year. That's an absolute saving of 6.85%, or a more worthwhile proportionate saving of 21.1%.

Those whose taxable income may fall into the highest marginal tax bracket of £100,000 to £125,140 next year may be able to make even greater savings. (As we saw in Chapter 2, dividends falling into this tax bracket in 2022/23 will be subject to effective marginal tax rates of between 50.625% and 56.25%)

For example, if you expect total taxable income of £75,000 in 2021/22 but £125,000 in 2022/23, taking an extra £25,000 of dividends this year will give you an extra Income Tax bill of £8,125 BUT, if this means you can take £25,000 less next year, it will save you between £12,656 and £14,063.

Another potential tax saving opportunity may arise if you expect your taxable income to be over £100,000 in each year and more than £225,140 over two years taken together. For example, if you expect taxable income of £125,140 in both 2021/22 and 2022/23, taking an extra £25,140 of dividends this year will give you an extra Income Tax bill of £8,186 BUT, if this means you can take £25,140 less next year, it will save you between £12,727 and £14,141, or a net saving over two years of between £4,541 and £5,955.

Those with income at this sort of level can continue to make significant savings every two years by keeping their taxable income to £100,000 in one year and taking any extra dividends they need in the next. A small company owner who pursues this 'rollercoaster income' strategy could enjoy the saving of up to £5,955 referred to above and up to a further £5,641 every two years thereafter (using 2022/23 tax rates).

Additional Rate Taxpayers

Company owners who can expect to be additional rate taxpayers every year will see very little benefit in taking additional dividends this year. The saving of 1.25% represents a proportionate saving of just 3.28%, hardly worth paying tax a year early for.

The only exception will be those adopting the 'rollercoaster income' strategy referred to above.

Management Accounts

Dividends must be paid out of distributable profits. If your latest statutory accounts do not show sufficient profits available, you can prepare a more up to date set of management accounts to demonstrate that the dividends you wish to take by 5th April 2022 are covered.

Chapter 9

Other Tax Year End Planning

Key Date to Take Action by: 5th April 2022

As we have seen, the cost of employment will rise by 2.5% in most cases from 6th April 2022. It is seldom worth making extra payments just to save tax, and certainly not to save a mere 2.5%, but sometimes it is worth accelerating the payments you are going to make anyway.

Some employers make non-contractual bonus payments to their staff. If you intend to do this in the near future, it is worth doing it by 5th April 2022 in order to avoid the National Insurance increases.

In Chapter 4, we looked at tax-efficient salaries for owner/directors. Whatever salary works best for you in 2021/22. Make sure you pay it by 5th April.

Tax-efficient salary payments to your spouse or other family members should also be considered by 5th April.

In Chapter 5, we looked at the tax saving opportunities provided by borrowing from your company. If you intend to do this in the near future, it will be better to borrow the money by 5th April 2022 so that your company pays Section 455 tax at 32.5% and not 33.75%.

Chapter 10

Company Year End Planning

Key Date to Take Action by: Your Company's Next Accounting Date, OR the One after That

Take a look at Appendix B and you will see how much your company's Corporation Tax rate will increase over the next couple of years. In terms of when this increase will bite, we can effectively divide companies into three categories:

i. Companies with annual profits not exceeding £50,000*: you will not see any increase in your Corporation Tax rate

ii. Companies with annual profits of more than £50,000* and a 31st March accounting date: an increase of either 6% or 7.5% in your marginal Corporation Tax rate will hit you all in one go on 1st April 2023

iii. Companies with annual profits of more than £50,000* and a different accounting date: a total increase of either 6% or 7.5% in your marginal Corporation Tax rate will hit you in two stages, firstly in the accounting period that straddles 31st March 2023 (your next accounting period in many cases); with the remaining increase applying in the following accounting period

* Less if the company has any associated companies: see Chapter 2.

Companies in categories (ii) and (iii) may be able to make Corporation Tax savings by accelerating taxable profits or capital gains on disposals of company assets; or by deferring tax deductible expenditure. This form of planning is of no benefit to companies in category (i).

The best savings of 6% or 7.5% are available to companies in category (ii) and these companies need to take action by 31st March 2023 to benefit.

The position for companies in category (iii) is a little more complex as the savings are spread over two years. The example of Timdal Ltd in Chapter 3 provides a good illustration. For these companies there are potentially two key dates to take action by: your next accounting date after 31st March 2022; and your following accounting date falling a year later.

Whether it is worth taking any of the action discussed below will depend on many factors, including your company's accounting date, profit level, and financial position. Of paramount importance is that the action must not have a detrimental impact on the company's business. Commercial considerations must take precedence.

Accelerating Taxable Income and Gains

The happy coincidence the increase in Corporation Tax rates brings is that it will both save tax **and** make commercial sense to accelerate income so that it falls into an earlier accounting period.

So, get out there and sell! Well, that's obvious, but what else should you consider as you get close to one of those critical accounting dates (broadly any accounting date between April 2022 and February 2024). Here are some possible steps:

- Complete orders and projects and bring billing up to date. Accounting rules often require part-completed work to be brought into account, but there is still a large element of profit dependent on completion and billing in many cases. For example, two half completed projects are, in accounting terms, likely to yield less profit than a single completed project of the same size.

- Connected businesses (e.g. wife has her own company, husband also has his own business): make extra sales to connected businesses in advance of the company's accounting date.

It may also be worth considering accelerating the disposal of a company asset where this may lead to a significant capital gain.

Example

Lotlen Ltd is a property investment company with a portfolio of residential rental properties. It draws up accounts to 31ˢᵗ March each year and generally makes an annual profit of around £75,000. Lotlen Ltd is planning to sell one of its investment properties and anticipates this will yield a taxable capital gain of £150,000. If the sale takes place by 31ˢᵗ March 2023, the Corporation Tax arising on the capital gain will be £28,500 (£150,000 x 19%).

However, if the sale takes place after 31ˢᵗ March 2023, the Corporation Tax arising on the gain will be £39,750 (£150,000 x 26.5%).

Hence, making sure the sale takes place by 31ˢᵗ March 2023 will save the company £11,250 (£39,750 – £28,500).

Deferring Expenditure

Companies must prepare accounts on an accruals basis (sometimes called generally accepted accounting principles, or 'GAAP'), so simply deferring payment does not make any difference to the company's taxable profits. What is needed is to defer when the expenditure is actually incurred. This isn't possible with some items, like Business Rates, electricity, or bank interest. Nonetheless, expenditure that can sometimes be deferred includes:

- Repairs and maintenance (where there is some discretion over timing)
- Advertising and promotion
- Travel and subsistence (by altering the timing of business journeys)
- Employee bonuses (where these are discretionary or gratuitous, rather than contractual): but see also Chapter 7 regarding the forthcoming National Insurance increases
- Staff entertaining (other entertaining is not tax deductible, so the timing of it won't alter your Corporation Tax bill)
- Staff recruitment (agents' commission will generally be a deductible expense)
- Pension contributions (see Chapter 5 for further details)
- Legal and professional costs, such as business advice, or consultancy (provided these are not regular, annual costs that would be recognised in the accounts in any case)

As far as capital expenditure is concerned, there are other tax implications to be considered, so we will look at these in Chapter 11.

Accounting Adjustments

Carefully considered accounting adjustments can slightly alter the timing of company profits. While accounts must be prepared on a reasonable, 'true and fair' basis, there is often some leeway in the exact amount of each accounting adjustment. With most companies' marginal Corporation Tax rates set to increase, it may make sense to maximise profits in the last accounting period before the Corporation Tax increase begins to take effect.

Of course, it is only worth increasing the profits taxed at 19% if the relevant accounting adjustments will subsequently reverse and thus reduce profits in later accounting periods.

Unlike accelerating actual income there is no 'happy coincidence' here. Accounting adjustments that lead to an increase in current taxable profits will have a negative cashflow impact. But you may, for example, consider it worth paying £1,900 more on 1st January 2024 in order to pay £2,650 less on 1st January 2025. I make that a very respectable return of 39.5%.

Changing the Company's Accounting Date

Some company owners might consider changing their company's accounting date in order to defer the impact of the Corporation Tax increase.

Generally, I would say this is not worthwhile, but there may be exceptions where the company has an unusually high level of taxable profits or capital gains in the last few months before 31st March 2023.

Example
Gerfro Ltd has drawn up accounts to 31st December for many years. It generally makes annual profits of around £100,000. However, in February 2023, it disposes of a property and makes a taxable capital gain of £250,000.

If the company carries on as it is, the Corporation Tax arising on its capital gain will effectively be:

£149,317 @ 24.651% =	*£36,808*
£100,683 @ 23.521% =	*£23,682*
Total	*£60,490*

(See Appendix B for the Corporation Tax rates and thresholds used here)

Alternatively, if the company changes its accounting date and draws up accounts for the fifteen months ending 31st March 2023, the Corporation Tax on its capital gain, at 19%, will be £47,500.

A simple change of accounting date has saved this company £12,990!

Chapter 11

Timing Capital Expenditure

Key Date to Take Action by: Your Company's Next Accounting Date, the One after That, OR 31st March 2023

For most small companies, deferring capital expenditure on used or second-hand 'plant and machinery' will generally have the same potentially beneficial impact as we looked at in Chapter 10 for other items. However, there are some important exceptions and other additional factors to be aware of.

Plant and machinery includes machinery, furniture, equipment, software, motorcycles, commercial vehicles, and even robots (see Chapter 7). For a more detailed definition, see the Taxcafe.co.uk guide *'The Company Tax Changes'*.

Cars

Cars do not qualify for either the super-deduction or the annual investment allowance (see below). Most cars only attract writing down allowances at either 6% or 18%, so deferring car purchases will not lead to any worthwhile Corporation Tax savings. The exception to this exception is new electric cars, which currently qualify for a 100% allowance. This allowance will be reviewed in the next few years and may be withdrawn at some future date. This would obviously make it disadvantageous to delay the purchase beyond the date of withdrawal.

The Super-Deduction

Purchases of **new** (and only new), qualifying plant and machinery made by companies between 1st April 2021 and 31st March 2023 qualify for a super-deduction of up to 130%.

There are a number of exclusions to be aware of, the main ones being cars (as usual), integral features (see below), and assets held for leasing (this does not generally apply to fixtures and fittings within commercial property).

For company accounting periods spanning 31st March 2023, the super-deduction is given at a reduced rate, but still applies to purchases made by that date. For earlier accounting periods, the full 130% deduction applies.

The overall impact of the super-deduction is that, for companies with annual profits in excess of £250,000, but not spending in excess of the annual investment allowance (see below), there is generally very little difference in the amount of Corporation Tax saved whenever new qualifying plant and machinery is purchased (the saving will vary between 24.7% and 25.3%, depending on the company's accounting period). However, this is subject to the important exception arising under point (ii) below.

For a detailed analysis of the super-deduction and the tax planning implications arising, see the Taxcafe.co.uk guide *The Company Tax Changes*. However, the following points summarise the position:

i. Companies spending in excess of the annual investment allowance will benefit by purchasing new qualifying plant and machinery by 31st March 2023

ii. Companies with annual profits of more than £50,000* and accounting periods spanning 31st March 2023 should generally try to avoid purchasing new qualifying plant and machinery between 1st April 2023 and their next accounting date thereafter: as these purchases will not qualify for the super-deduction, and nor will they provide the higher rate of Corporation Tax relief that will apply in later accounting periods

iii. Companies with annual profits of £50,000* or less will benefit by purchasing new qualifying plant and machinery before 1st April 2023, and will benefit most by making their purchases in an accounting period ending before that date

iv. Subject to point (i), companies with annual profits of more than £50,000* but no more than £250,000* will benefit most by deferring purchases of qualifying plant and machinery until an accounting period beginning after 31st March 2023. However, subject to point (ii), the saving on purchases of new qualifying plant and machinery will only amount to 1.8% at most

* Reduced if the company has any associated companies: see Chapter 2.

Integral Features

The following items are classed as integral features:

- Electrical lighting and power systems
- Cold water systems
- Space or water heating systems, air conditioning, ventilation and air purification systems and floors or ceilings comprised in such systems
- Lifts, escalators and moving walkways
- External solar shading

Purchases of new integral features (including those acquired as part of the purchase of a new, previously unused, building) within commercial property, made by companies between 1st April 2021 and 31st March 2023, qualify for a 50% first year allowance.

Where the company is spending in excess of the annual investment allowance, it will therefore make sense to make these purchases by 31st March 2023.

A more detailed analysis of the 50% first year allowance and the tax planning implications arising is again provided in the Taxcafe.co.uk guide *'The Company Tax Changes'*.

Other Property Expenditure

Apart from integral features, most other fixtures and fittings within commercial property will qualify as plant and machinery and will attract the same capital allowances, including the super-deduction for new items.

However, the building itself will either attract no allowances at all, or a 3% annual structures and buildings allowance.

Hence, deferring expenditure on buildings will not lead to any Corporation Tax savings (not for over thirty years, anyway).

For further information regarding capital allowances on property, and assets within property, see the Taxcafe.co.uk guides *'Using a Property Company to Save Tax'* and *'How to Save Property Tax'*.

The Annual Investment Allowance

Companies are currently entitled to an annual investment allowance of up to £1m. This limit was due to fall to just £200,000 from 1st January 2021, but the reduction in the limit has twice been postponed and is now scheduled to take place on 1st April 2023.

The annual investment allowance provides 100% tax relief for qualifying expenditure on plant and machinery (whether new or second hand) up to the specified limit in each accounting period. Expenditure qualifying for the super-deduction does not use up any of the company's annual investment allowance.

Transitional rules apply where a company's accounting period spans the change in the limit on 1st April 2023. In these cases, the maximum annual investment allowance is calculated on a pro rata basis.

For example, a company with a twelve month accounting period ending 31st December 2023 is entitled to a maximum annual investment allowance for the whole year of:

90/365 x £1m	£246,575
275/365 x £200,000	£150,685
Total:	£397,260

But, an additional rule applies to expenditure incurred after 31st March 2023. The maximum amount that can be claimed in respect of expenditure incurred in the part of the accounting period falling after that date is restricted to the appropriate proportion of the £200,000 limit.

Hence, in the case of the company described above, the maximum annual investment allowance that could be claimed on expenditure incurred between 1st April and 31st December 2023 is just £150,685.

The maximum annual investment allowance applying for other twelve month accounting periods straddling 1st April 2023 is as set out in the table below. This is given in two parts, the maximum for the year as a whole, and the maximum for the period from 1st April 2023 to the end of the accounting period ('After 31-Mar-2023').

Year ending	Maximum annual investment allowance	
	Whole Year	**After 31-Mar-2023**
30-Apr-2023	£934,247	£16,438
31-May-2023	£866,301	£33,425
30-Jun-2023	£800,548	£49,863
31-Jul-2023	£732,603	£66,849
31-Aug-2023	£664,658	£83,836
30-Sep-2023	£598,904	£100,274
31-Oct-2023	£530,959	£117,260
30-Nov-2023	£465,205	£133,699
31-Dec-2023	£397,260	£150,685
31-Jan-2024	£329,315	£167,671
29-Feb-2024	£267,760	£183,060

Remembering also that expenditure incurred after 31st March 2023 will not qualify for the super-deduction, it will be important for many companies with accounting periods spanning that date to purchase most of their qualifying plant and machinery by 31st March 2023. While the new £200,000 limit will be enough for the majority of small companies, the transitional rules described above may catch some people out!

Chapter 12

Is It Still Worth It?

With all the tax increases facing owner/directors and their companies over the next few years, some small company owners may be wondering if it is still worth operating through a company.

Having looked at the figures, my view is that, subject to a few quirks here and there, operating through a company will remain broadly as worthwhile in future as it is today: namely it will be worthwhile where the business is making a reasonable level of profit and the owner leaves a reasonable proportion of the after tax profits in the company.

Before we look at the figures though, it's worth remembering there are other good reasons for operating through a company, apart from annual tax savings. Companies provide limited liability protection, greater flexibility for the ownership structure, and opportunities for succession planning.

On the other hand, the administration and accounting costs (and management time) involved in using a company will generally be greater, so it's only worthwhile if the tax savings are significant or there are other compelling reasons to use a company.

The Figures

In the tables below, we will compare the tax burden on a sole trader with that on a company and its director in the current tax year and the next two years at different profit levels.

To begin with, we will look at the position where the owner/director withdraws all the company's after tax profits. As we know from Chapter 4, where the director has no other income, the most tax efficient way to do this will generally be to take a salary equal to the National Insurance primary threshold and the remainder as dividends, so that is what is assumed here.

Sole Trader versus Company: Tax Suffered 2021/22

Profit	Sole Trader	Company	Saving/(Cost)
£30,000	£5,483	£4,823	£660
£40,000	£8,383	£7,331	£1,053
£50,000	£11,283	£9,838	£1,445
£60,000	£15,448	£12,363	£3,086
£80,000	£23,848	£21,428	£2,421
£100,000	£32,248	£30,493	£1,756
£125,000	£47,748	£42,309	£5,439
£150,000	£58,276	£58,008	£268
£200,000	£81,776	£81,868	(£92)
£250,000	£105,276	£106,799	(£1,522)

Sole Trader versus Company: Tax Suffered 2022/23

Profit	Sole Trader	Company	Saving/(Cost)
£30,000	£5,712	£4,925	£787
£40,000	£8,737	£7,534	£1,203
£50,000	£11,762	£10,143	£1,619
£60,000	£16,052	£12,779	£3,273
£80,000	£24,702	£22,047	£2,655
£100,000	£33,352	£31,314	£2,038
£125,000	£49,165	£43,411	£5,754
£150,000	£60,005	£59,419	£586
£200,000	£84,130	£83,778	£352
£250,000	£108,255	£109,214	(£959)

Sole Trader versus Company: Tax Suffered 2023/24

Profit	Sole Trader	Company	Saving/(Cost)
£30,000	£5,675	£4,868	£807
£40,000	£8,700	£7,477	£1,223
£50,000	£11,725	£10,085	£1,639
£60,000	£16,015	£12,738	£3,277
£80,000	£24,665	£22,981	£1,684
£100,000	£33,315	£33,242	£73
£125,000	£49,127	£46,069	£3,059
£150,000	£59,968	£62,374	(£2,406)
£200,000	£84,093	£90,132	(£6,039)
£250,000	£108,218	£117,843	(£9,625)

Notes

1. The sole trader's tax burden comprises Income Tax, Class 2 and Class 4 National Insurance and, in 2023/24, the Health and Social Care Levy.

2. The 'Company' tax burden includes Corporation Tax, employer's National Insurance (including the Health and Social Care Levy element in 2023/24) and Income Tax paid by the director.

3. Company profit is before paying the director's salary and related employer's National Insurance.

4. It is assumed the business owner has no other taxable income.

5. Inflationary increases (at 3.5%) have been assumed for both National Insurance thresholds in 2023/24.

6. It is assumed the employment allowance is not available to cover National Insurance arising on the director's salary.

7. In practice, it will not generally be possible to withdraw all profits from the company in the same tax year as they are earned, as dividends must be paid out of accumulated reserves. However, the tables still serve as an illustration of the long-term position where this strategy is being pursued.

Summary So Far

At present, an owner/director who withdraws all their after tax profits from the company each year can make reasonable savings where their business makes annual profits between around £60,000 and £125,000. In 2022/23 those savings will improve but, in 2023/24, this strategy will only be worthwhile in a few cases. In fact, as we can see from the last table, at high profit levels following this strategy will prove quite costly in future.

Retaining Profits in the Company

But, as I said above, companies are most worthwhile when a reasonable proportion of the annual profits are being retained in the company. The more profit retained the more beneficial it is to use a company.

The following tables are based on the same assumptions as above, including Notes 1 to 6 but, instead of the company owner withdrawing all their after tax profits, they take a salary equal to the National Insurance primary threshold and then take dividends equal to 75% of the company's profit after tax. (For this purpose, profit after tax is also after the director's salary and related employer's National Insurance.)

Sole Trader versus Company: Tax Suffered 2021/22
(25% of After Tax Profit Retained in Company)

Profit	Sole Trader	Company	Saving
£30,000	£5,483	£4,515	£969
£40,000	£8,383	£6,870	£1,513
£50,000	£11,283	£9,226	£2,058
£60,000	£15,448	£11,582	£3,867
£80,000	£23,848	£16,799	£7,049
£100,000	£32,248	£24,548	£7,701
£125,000	£47,748	£34,234	£13,515
£150,000	£58,276	£43,920	£14,357
£200,000	£81,776	£68,573	£13,204
£250,000	£105,276	£88,256	£17,020

Sole Trader versus Company: Tax Suffered 2022/23
(25% of After Tax Profit Retained in Company)

Profit	Sole Trader	Company	Saving
£30,000	£5,712	£4,571	£1,141
£40,000	£8,737	£7,002	£1,735
£50,000	£11,762	£9,434	£2,328
£60,000	£16,052	£11,865	£4,187
£80,000	£24,702	£17,263	£7,439
£100,000	£33,352	£25,163	£8,189
£125,000	£49,165	£35,039	£14,125
£150,000	£60,005	£44,915	£15,090
£200,000	£84,130	£70,020	£14,110
£250,000	£108,255	£90,090	£18,165

Sole Trader versus Company: Tax Suffered 2023/24
(25% of After Tax Profit Retained in Company)

Profit	Sole Trader	Company	Saving/(Cost)
£30,000	£5,675	£4,520	£1,155
£40,000	£8,700	£6,952	£1,748
£50,000	£11,725	£9,383	£2,342
£60,000	£16,015	£11,815	£4,200
£80,000	£24,665	£18,346	£6,319
£100,000	£33,315	£27,367	£5,948
£125,000	£49,127	£38,643	£10,484
£150,000	£59,968	£49,919	£10,048
£200,000	£84,093	£76,168	£7,925
£250,000	£108,218	£100,419	£7,799

Conclusion

Where a reasonable proportion of profits are retained in the company, a company is worthwhile in all tax years at any profit level over around £50,000.

Some Final Points

The tables above are based on a single owner/director. Where there are two or more owner/directors the position will be different, although the overall conclusions will be broadly the same.

In this chapter, I have examined the position for trading businesses. For a detailed look at the position for property letting businesses, see the Taxcafe.co.uk guide *'Using a Property Company to Save Tax'*.

Appendix A

UK Tax Rates and Allowances: 2020/21 to 2022/23

	Rates	2020/21 £	2021/22 £	2022/23 £
Income Tax (1)				
Personal allowance		12,500	12,570	12,570
Basic rate band	20%	37,500	37,700	37,700
Higher rate/Threshold	40%	50,000	50,270	50,270
Personal allowance withdrawal				
Effective rate/From	60%	100,000	100,000	100,000
To		125,000	125,140	125,140
Additional rate	45%	150,000	150,000	150,000
Starting rate band (2)	0%	5,000	5,000	5,000
Personal savings allowance (3)		1,000	1,000	1,000
Dividend allowance		2,000	2,000	2,000
Marriage allowance (4)		1,250	1,260	1,260
National Insurance				
Primary Threshold		9,500	9,568	9,880
Rate: Self-Employed (Class 4)		9%	9%	10.25%
Employees (Class 1)		12%	12%	13.25%
Upper earnings limit (UEL)		50,000	50,270	50,270
Rate above UEL		2%	2%	3.25%
Secondary Threshold		8,788	8,840	9,100
Rate: Employers		13.8%	13.8%	15.05%
Employment allowance		4,000	4,000	4,000
Class 2 per week		3.05	3.05	3.15
Small profits threshold		6,475	6,515	6,725
Capital Gains Tax				
Annual exemption		12,300	12,300	12,300
Inheritance Tax				
Nil rate band		325,000	325,000	325,000
Main residence nil rate band		175,000	175,000	175,000
Annual Exemption		3,000	3,000	3,000

Notes
1. Different rates and thresholds apply to Scottish taxpayers (except on interest, savings, and dividend income, and on capital gains)
2. Applies to interest and savings income only
3. £500 higher rate taxpayers; not available to additional rate taxpayers
4. Available where neither spouse/civil partner pays higher rate tax

Marginal Corporation Tax Rates 2018 to 2024

Year Ending:	Small Profits Rate	Marginal Rate	Main Rate
31-Mar-2018 to 31-Mar-2023	n/a	n/a	19.000%
30-Apr-2023	19.000%	19.616%	19.493%
31-May-2023	19.000%	20.253%	20.003%
30-Jun-2023	19.000%	20.870%	20.496%
31-Jul-2023	19.000%	21.507%	21.005%
31-Aug-2023	19.000%	22.144%	21.515%
30-Sep-2023	19.000%	22.760%	22.008%
31-Oct-2023	19.000%	23.397%	22.518%
30-Nov-2023	19.000%	24.014%	23.011%
31-Dec-2023	19.000%	24.651%	23.521%
31-Jan-2024	19.000%	25.288%	24.030%
29-Feb-2024	19.000%	25.865%	24.492%
31-Mar-2024	19.000%	26.500%	25.000%

Due to a quirk created by the leap year in 2024, for twelve month accounting periods ending between 1st April 2023 and 28th February 2024, the small profits rate will apply to profits up to £49,863; the marginal rate will apply to profits between £49,863 and £249,317; and the main rate will apply to profits over £249,317.

For twelve month accounting periods ending on any date from 29th February 2024 onwards, the small profits rate will apply to profits up to £50,000; the marginal rate will apply to profits between £50,000 and £250,000; and the main rate will apply to profits over £250,000.

As explained in Chapter 2, these limits are reduced where there are any associated companies.

Lightning Source UK Ltd.
Milton Keynes UK
UKHW021409190122
397396UK00004B/191